COUNTDOWN TO COLLAPSE

IRAN'S REGIME ON THE BRINK

STRUAN STEVENSON

COUNTDOWN TO COLLAPSE
IRAN'S REGIME ON THE BRINK

Copyright © Struan Stevenson, 2025

All rights reserved. No part of this book may be reproduced or used in any manner without proper attribution to the author.

To request permissions, contact the publisher at
https://isjcommittee.com/contact/

First published in July 2025
The International Committee in Search of Justice (ISJ)

ISBN: 9798292823735 (Paperback)

https://www.isjcommittee.com

The easiest way to establish a dictatorship is to claim you are God's representative on earth.

Christopher Hitchens

ACKNOWLEDGEMENTS

My special thanks to my great friends and freedom fighters of many decades Alejo Vidal-Quadras, Former Vice-President of the European Parliament and Paulo Casaca, for their guidance and unfailing wisdom in the preparation of this book.

Struan Stevenson
Chair, Committee on the Protection of Political Freedoms in Iran, International Committee 'In Search of Justice' (ISJ)
Coordinator of the Campaign for Iran Change (CIC)
Glasgow, Scotland, July 2025

CONTENTS

Preface - Struan Stevenson

Foreword - Professor Ivan Sascha Sheehan

Chapter One - The Overthrow of The Shah................ 1

Chapter Two - How Ayatollah Ruhollah Khomeini Hijacked The 1979 Revolution................................ 17

Chapter Three - Velãyat-e Faqih – A Toxic Philosophy.. 31

Chapter Four - The War with Iraq........................... 49

Chapter Five - Why the IRGC Must be Blacklisted and Dismantled.. 63

Chapter Six - The Rise and Fall of Qassem Soleimani.. 77

Chapter Seven - How Iran Managed to Control the Iraqi Militias... 89

Chapter Eight - Why Did Iran Support Bashar Al-Assad in Syria?.. 99

Chapter Nine - The Iranian Regime's Support for the Houthi Rebels In Yemen.. 115

Chapter Ten - The Genesis of Hezbollah in Lebanon.. 125

Chapter Eleven - Terrorism and Hostage Taking as Iranian State Policy... 137

Chapter Twelve - Iran's Nuclear Programme: A Web of Deception... 153

Chapter Thirteen - Iran's True Resistance: Busting Opposition Myths... 165

Chapter Fourteen - The Iranian Regime's Misinformation Campaign...................................... 179

Chapter Fifteen - A Puppet in Power: Pezeshkian and the Supreme Leader's Script.................................. 179

Chapter Sixteen - From Protest to Revolution: The Rise of Resistance in Iran.. 209

Chapter Seventeen - The Final Reckoning: Iran at the Edge of Change.. 227

PREFACE

This book was written just before the recent twelve-day war erupted—a conflict that has since altered many regional and global assessments and introduced a fundamentally new reality. Yet, far from diminishing the book's core thesis, these developments have only reinforced and rendered it more urgent. The central argument of the book is built on two key propositions:

First: The religious dictatorship ruling Iran is the principal source of war, insecurity, and instability in the region. Its overthrow is a prerequisite for establishing peace and stability—not only in the Middle East, but also globally.

Second: Achieving this objective is not possible through foreign military intervention, nor through appeasement of the ruling theocracy. Real change can only come about through the Iranian people and their organized resistance.

If anything, the outbreak and consequences of the 12-day war have powerfully vindicated both propositions.

In June 2025, with the eruption of war between Israel and Iran and the entry of the United States, the conflict in the Middle East entered a new era unseen in the past four decades. After 10 days of Israeli airstrikes on nuclear sites, as well as on military commanders and compounds of the Islamic Revolutionary Guard Corps (IRGC) and other targets, and the Iranian regime's reciprocal missile fire on Tel Aviv and other centres in various Israeli cities, many feared the triggering of a much larger conflict. Although the United States exacerbated those fears by launching a large-scale attack on three regime nuclear sites, a ceasefire was established within 48 hours. Despite the blows inflicted on the mullahs' nuclear programme, the focal point of the Middle East problem, the situation regarding the Iranian regime, remains unresolved. Change in Iran is more necessary and accessible than ever, but the power of change is in the hands of the Iranian people alone.

There's a famous saying: "You have to know the past to understand the present." The rapidly escalating crisis in Iran has echoes right back to the earliest weeks of the fundamentalist Islamic Republic. Following the overthrow of the Shah in 1979, Ayatollah Ruhollah Khomeini hijacked the popular revolution and laid the foundations for his own vicious tyranny. The Iranian people soon realized the pitfall of swapping the savage autocracy of the hated Shah for the cruel, fundamentalist oppression of the mullahs. They realized they had jumped from the frying pan into the fire.

A massive uprising took place on June 20, 1981. Half a million protesters, organized by the People's Mojahedin of Iran/Mujahedin-e Khalq (PMOI or

MEK), rose up against Khomeini and against his nascent Islamic Republic and its toxic *Velāyat-e faqih*, or 'guardianship of the Islamic jurist,' constitution.

Undeterred, from that day to the present, the regime's executioners began their diligent work, torturing and executing thousands including more than 30,000 political prisoners during the infamous 1988 massacre, an atrocity described by the UN Special Rapporteur on Iran in a 2024 report as a crime against humanity and genocide.[1]

Today, the mullahs' theocratic regime teeters on the edge of the precipice. Their so-called 'axis of resistance' that included Hamas in Gaza, Hezbollah in Lebanon, the Houthis in Yemen and Bashar al-Assad in Syria, has collapsed. In a twelve-day war in June 2025, Israel and America joined in a calculated assault on the regime's nuclear sites. At least 30 senior commanders of Islamic Revolutionary Guard Corps (IRGC) and key nuclear scientists were eliminated. The 86-year-old Supreme Leader Ayatollah Ali Khamenei must truly regret his decision to train, finance and direct the horrific 7th October 2023 terrorist Hamas attack on Israel that triggered the

---

[1] Office of the United Nations High Commissioner for Human Rights (OHCHR), "Report of the Special Rapporteur on the situation of human rights in the Islamic Republic of Iran," 17 July 2024. Available at: https://www.ohchr.org/sites/default/files/documents/countries/iran/20240717-SR-Iran-Findings.pdf

Middle East conflict that has raged ever since and finally engulfed Iran itself. As the famous adage goes, "Those who sow the wind, shall reap the whirlwind."

Khamenei's years of sponsoring international terrorism and warmongering, while trying to persuade the West that he was only enriching uranium for peaceful, civilian energy purposes, have now spectacularly imploded. The United Nations' nuclear watchdog - The International Atomic Energy Agency (IAEA) - noted that Iran had a stockpile of around 900 lbs of uranium enriched to near weapons' grade - 60% purity. Uranium enriched for civilian energy purposes needs only to reach 4%. With the mullahs chanting "Death to America" and "Death to Israel", the theocratic regime's development of nuclear bombs and ballistic missile delivery systems was never going to be tolerated.

The mullahs, enmeshed in corruption and incompetence, have squandered the nation's wealth on funding terror and proxy militias. The Iranian economy now lies in ruins, strangled by mismanagement and the burden of sanctions. Billions have been wasted on the clandestine nuclear bomb and ballistic missile programme that is now a smouldering ruin. Iran's 90 million citizens have lost their fear of the mullahs and their savagery.

The exponential rise of PMOI Resistance Units across the nation has demonstrated the courage of the opposition, daily spraying anti-regime graffiti on the walls of public buildings, firebombing IRGC and Basij compounds, torching the regime's symbols, and displaying banners of NCRI leaders like Maryam Rajavi, placards declaring: "Down with the oppressor, be it the shah or the mullahs" and "No to the crown, no to the turban, the mullahs' time is over," are appearing regularly on the regime's bridges and buildings across Iran.

The rejection of the restoration of the monarchy by the Iranian people, exposes the efforts of the mullahs to claim that their removal will simply pave the way for Reza Pahlavi - the son of the deposed and hated Shah, to reclaim the Peacock Throne and restore fascist autocracy. After years of silence, the self-proclaimed 'Crown Prince' has suddenly re-emerged from his languid life of Western luxury, paid for by the billions looted by his father, to announce that he is the answer to the Iranian crisis. It is clear that he is being exploited as a 'useful idiot' by the mullahs' to confuse the rising tide of dissidents demanding regime change.

Incredibly, Pahlavi told a press conference in Paris on 23 June 2025 that he was in direct communication with the IRGC – the regime's Gestapo-like enforcers - which he sees as necessary not only to affect change but also to maintain order after the overthrow of the mullahs. He said that he is establishing: "a formal channel for military, security, and police personnel to reach out directly to me, my team, and our expanding operation." He claimed: "I know these officers, these soldiers, these brave men exist because they are reaching out to me and telling me they want to be part of this national salvation. But now, greater coordination is needed."

Describing members of the IRGC and Basij as "brave men" will have deeply outraged the tens of thousands of families of those who have been arrested, tortured and murdered by the mullahs' repressive forces. It is no wonder that the people of Iran reject both the current criminal theocracy and the past cruel monarchy.

Western appeasers must now end their wearisome calls for diplomacy and negotiation with this most vicious of regimes. It is time to show the Iranian people that the West backs their right to overthrow the mullahs and restore peace and prosperity to Iran and the Middle East. The Resistance Units illuminate the path to liberation, and the world waits to witness the dawn of a new era.

Struan Stevenson
Glasgow, Scotland
July 2025

FOREWORD

This compelling book, authored by a distinguished former member of the European Parliament and a tireless advocate for peace and democracy, is a timely call to the international community to reassess its engagement with the Iranian regime.

Struan Stevenson's narrative unfolds with a rigorous examination of two dictatorships that have shaped Iran's historical and political landscape: the autocratic monarchy of Mohammad Reza Pahlavi, which fell in the tumult of 1979, and the theocratic regime established by Ayatollah Khomeini. Khomeini's seizing of the revolution was not merely a coup against the Iranian people, rather, it constituted a shrewd stratagem to entrench a repressive theocracy that starkly contradicted the very aspirations for freedom and democracy that had ignited the anti-monarchical revolutionary fervour in the first place.

This book offers a meticulous critique of Khomeini's doctrine of *Velãyat-e faqih* (absolute clerical rule), the engine for centralising authority among a select cadre of fundamentalist clerics and their corrupt underlings. This doctrine not only institutionalises misogyny and systemic discrimination but also dismantles the foundations of democratic governance. It fosters a pervasive culture of fear and silencing dissent, thus systematically undermining the fundamental rights of people in Iran. Still, this examination not only critiques the historical trajectory of Iran but also serves as a poignant reminder of the enduring and courageous struggle for human rights and dignity against the clerical regime.

Stevenson's analysis of the Iran-Iraq War in the 1980s provides a compelling lens into the regime's role in igniting and sustaining this prolonged conflict, which inflicted a catastrophic toll on both sides. His account uncovers how the Iranian regime callously sacrificed countless lives as cannon fodder in order to advance an expansionist agenda with deep, troubling implications for regional stability.

Interwoven within this narrative is a profound study of figures like Qassem Soleimani, the former commander of the Islamic Revolutionary Guard Corps' (IRGC) Quds Force. Stevenson presents Soleimani not simply as a military leader but as an architect of regional destabilisation, leveraging a network of terrorism and proxy warfare to project the theocracy's malign influence. Soleimani's legacy illustrates the Iranian regime's reliance on fear and violence and its inherent inability to reform its behaviour. Stevenson's insights here provide a vital understanding of the regime's motivations and a sombre warning about the lasting consequences of their pursuit.

With this foundation established, Stevenson's illuminating account is not merely a chronicle of the threats posed by Iran's theocracy, it is a strategic blueprint for dismantling those threats and empowering the forces of change. It provides a compelling answer to the question: "How can we cut this Gordian Knot?"

The reader will discover a piercing critique of past and current Western policies that, for decades, have rested upon the shaky foundations of appeasement. This has been a perilous strategy that has consistently failed to curb the Iranian regime's belligerence and, in fact, has often emboldened it, thus raising the prospects of a military conflict. Stevenson expertly traces a history of misguided overtures rooted in the hope that dialogue and engagement might temper the regime's actions. Echoing Winston Churchill's timeless warning, "An appeaser is one who feeds a crocodile, hoping it will eat him last," Stevenson argues that the Iranian regime has adroitly exploited each diplomatic overture to consolidate power domestically while expanding its disruptive influence across the region.

Relying on these important lessons, the book makes an urgent case for a dramatic yet immeasurably more rational strategic pivot. It underscores that a reliance on conventional diplomatic approaches in addressing the Iranian regime's threats is not only ineffectual but counterproductive, serving to exacerbate conflict and heighten the risk of further bloodshed. We know this because the regime has repeatedly demonstrated that it views concessions as signs of weakness, seizing on diplomatic overtures to fortify its political and military apparatus and accelerate its damaging designs. In typical fashion, the fall of Assad has sparked a renewed flurry of appeasement from Western leaders. There is an emerging narrative that the destruction of Hamas and Hezbollah and Assad's departure has so weakened the Iranian regime that the West must now negotiate with the so called 'moderate' president Masoud Pezeshkian to abandon his country's nuclear ambitions and restore peace and harmony to the Middle East.

How utterly foolish.

Pezeshkian is no moderate. He is a puppet of the Supreme Leader who carries out his orders blindly. Since taking office in August 2024, in less than 12 months he presided over the execution of more than 1,200 people, including dozens of women and seven juvenile offenders.[2] Barbarically, 7 of the hangings were carried out in public in an attempt to terrify the rebellious youth into placid submission. Public hangings are generally from a construction crane, an especially slow and agonizing execution method.

---

[2] "22 Prisoners Executed Between December 24-26," NCRI, 26 December 2024. Available at: https://www.ncri-iran.org/en/ncri-statements/statement-human-rights/iran-22-prisoners-executed-between-december-24-26-28-year-old-dies-in-evin/

According to Amnesty International, the number of executions in Iran in 2023 accounted for approximately 74% of all documented executions worldwide. [3]That record has been surpassed in 2024 and 2025. Undeterred, the regime began the New Year of 2025 with a fresh wave of hangings. On 1 March 2025, 27 people were executed. Ten prisoners were executed in the northeastern city of Mashhad, seven in Zahedan, in the southeast. Among those executed were 131 Baluchis, highlighting the disproportionate targeting of this marginalized and oppressed ethnic group.

The Iranian regime's involvement in the international drug trade has been known for years. Its elite Islamic Revolutionary Guard Corps (IRGC) maintains extensive mafia networks, laundering billions of dollars of dirty money for gangsters and cartel Godfathers, helping the mullahs to overcome the impact of western sanctions, and providing the regime with the means to finance and supply its terrorist proxies. Despite this well-known fact, more than half of those hanged (502 prisoners) were executed on drug-related charges. In Iran, drug charges are commonly used as cover for the execution of political prisoners, particularly members or supporters of the

---

[3] Amnesty International, "Global: Executions soar to highest number in almost a decade," 29 May 2024. Available at:
https://www.amnesty.org/en/latest/news/2024/05/global-executions-soar-highest-number-in-decade/

main democratic opposition movement, the Mujahedin-e Khalq (PMOI or MEK).

Part of the IRGC's narco-network was exposed after the fall of the Bashar al-Assad regime in Syria. His regime played a key role in the Captagon drug trade alongside Hezbollah. Captagon is an amphetamine-type stimulant widely misused in the Middle East. The US Treasury Department noted last year that Assad and his allies had "increasingly embraced the production and trafficking of Captagon to generate hard currency." Hezbollah were actively involved in supervising the building of a new Captagon factory in eastern Syria before Bashar al-Assad's ouster. They were being closely overseen by the IRGC.

The tumult of hangings is the tip of an iceberg of barbarism. The cruelty and inhumanity of Iran's judicial system goes well beyond executions. Individuals may be arrested and indefinitely detained without charge on trumped-up offences, and subjected to degrading treatment, including torture, in order to extract confessions. Those accused and/or convicted of perpetrating crimes are incarcerated in overcrowded prisons where they may be subject to torture, rape, and other atrocities. Iran's densely populated and dirty penitentiaries are also breeding grounds for COVID-19 and other illnesses, and prisoners are often denied necessary medical care, personal protective equipment, and disinfectant. Under the mullahs' 'justice' system they are denied rights such as access to legal counsel and a fair and speedy trial, and sentenced to other barbaric penalties such as amputation, blinding, and flogging.

In Urmia prison in West Azerbaijan province, the regime's Sharia courts ordered the amputation of the fingers of two brothers for the crime of petty theft. On January 2, 2025, a further 4 prisoners were hanged in Urmia Central prison. Two other prisoners had their fingers amputated in the main prison in the Holy City of Qom. The supposedly 'moderate' president, Masoud Pezeshkian, demonstrated his moderation by allowing the prisoners to be anaesthetised before their limbs were amputated! In another blatant crime against humanity, Khamenei's judiciary sentenced a political prisoner from the 2017 nationwide uprising to having his eyes gouged out, for allegedly blinding a State Security Force (SSF) officer by throwing a stone at him.

In a poignant Christmas 2024 letter smuggled out of the notorious Ghezel Hesar state prison in Karaj and written by a political prisoner called Saeed Masouri, now in his 25th year of incarceration, he recounted the relentless suffering and escalating executions under the Iranian regime. Masouri shared the heart-wrenching memories of lost cellmates taken to the gallows and the psychological scars of living under the constant threat of death, highlighting the human cost of a regime that executes one person every four hours on average.

Masouri's harrowing letter was addressed to international human rights authorities, including the UN Human Rights Council, the UN Secretary General, and the UN Special Rapporteur on the Human Rights Situation in Iran. Surely now is the time for them to act. The West can no longer close its eyes to the suffering and human rights abuse that continues daily in Iran. Khamenei and his hangmen must be consigned to the dustbin of history.

The primitive and ageing Supreme Leader, Ayatollah Ali Khamenei, has watched the gradual unravelling of his warmongering stranglehold in the region with the decapitation of his proxies, namely Hamas in Gaza and Hezbollah in Lebanon. The sudden and unexpected fall of Bashar al-Assad in Syria, the Islamic Republic's greatest ally, has sounded the death knell for the mullahs' regime. Now, Khamenei can only shudder at the arrival of the second presidency of Donald Trump, with his maximum pressure sanctions campaign and an unwavering antipathy to the Iranian regime's sponsorship of international terrorism.

Ever since the mullahs hijacked the popular revolution that ousted the dictatorship of the Shah in 1979, they have resorted to bouts of brutal repression at times of crisis to subdue the populace. But their atrocities only strengthen the determination of the Iranian youth to overthrow the fascist tyranny. The regime must be ostracised by the international community and any dealings with it should be conditional on an end to executions and torture. Its leaders must be brought to justice. There can no longer be a business-as-usual approach by Western appeasers. Too much innocent blood is being spilled as Khamenei sets new records for crimes and executions in a bid to delay his inevitable downfall.

Stevenson advocates for a more resolute and assertive international strategy, one that systematically erodes the regime's power while diminishing the likelihood of military confrontation. This approach is grounded in clarity, reality, and resolve. It is a paradigm that recognizes the Iranian people and their organized resistance as central to any successful strategic approach.

This book emphasises the importance of aligning with those committed to establishing a democratic, secular, and peaceful republic in Iran. This alignment is presented as a crucial step in fostering meaningful change and stability in the region. By engaging constructively with the organised opposition, the international community can contribute to a more favourable geopolitical landscape.

This shift, Stevenson contends, is not only a moral imperative but a strategic necessity. The West can help dismantle a system that has, time and again, relied on fear, repression, and terror. In this sense, Stevenson's analysis is as much a roadmap for a new policy direction as it is a sobering reminder of the high costs of past failures.

In what follows, we are urged to move beyond the simplistic dichotomy of engagement versus confrontation. There is, indeed, a third strategic path beyond this tired and false duality. This alternative rests on acknowledging the Iranian people as a crucial element in any sustainable plan for democratic regime change. The regime's hold is not invincible. Its Achilles' heel is the growing discontent among its own citizens. Integrating these forces into a broader geopolitical vision is essential for Western policymakers, who, in supporting this cause, can lay the groundwork for a peaceful future for the Middle East.

The stakes could not be higher. Iran's relentless policies of aggression and state-sponsored terror pose a direct threat to global security. Confronting this reality calls for a unified, resolute approach, one that transcends half-measures and diplomatic hesitancy. The message here is clear. Enduring stability in the Middle East cannot be achieved without addressing the fundamental issues posed by the Iranian regime. Only through a strategic, collective response can the international community lay the groundwork for a safer, more secure world.

We stand at a pivotal juncture in world history where authoritarianism is on the rise. The choices made today will cast long shadows over the geopolitical landscape for generations to come. By acknowledging the potential for transformation within Iran and actively supporting those who envision a democratic future, the international community can chart a resolute course against oppression and violent expansionism everywhere. This path demands both courage and tenacity. Yet the rewards – a world unburdened by the warmongering and emerging nuclear threats of a fundamentalist theocracy – are unquestionably worth the collective effort. Now, more than ever, is the moment to embody courage, and to embrace and support the Iranian people's quest for freedom. Our shared future depends on it.

Ivan Sascha Sheehan, Ph.D.
Associate Dean and Professor of Public and International Affairs
College of Public Affairs
University of Baltimore
Maryland

1

"Every revolution was first a thought in one man's mind."
- *Ralph Waldo Emerson*

THE OVERTHROW OF THE SHAH

A Dynasty of Desks: The Shah's Repressive Rule

Shah Mohammad Reza Pahlavi was the son of an illiterate and poor former soldier, Reza Khan,[1] who rose through the ranks of the Persian Cossack Brigade, a force trained and led by Russian officers in Iran and became a colonel. He became Minister of War after he staged a military a coup d'état in February 1921, orchestrated with British support. Seyyed Zia Tabatabaei became Prime Minister, while Reza Khan was appointed Minister of War before ultimately sidelining Zia and seizing power for himself. Reza Khan took over as prime minister and

---

[1] In *Mission for My Country*, Mohammad Reza Pahlavi himself reflects on his father, Reza Shah, describing him as "one of the most formidable men" he had ever encountered. The starkness of this characterization underscores the intimidation his father inspired, even within his own family.

gradually moved to assume the peacock throne and the vast wealth of the monarchy. On 12 December 1925, he officially declared himself the Shah (King) of Iran.

Reza Shah expressed admiration for aspects of Hitler's Nazi Germany, and ties between the two countries strengthened in the 1930s. In the book *Mémoires de Tadj ol-Molouk*,[2] both Reza Shah's wife and also mother recount a revealing episode from 1936, when a high-ranking Iranian delegation visited Nazi Germany and presented Adolf Hitler with two opulent Tabrizi carpets, one woven with Hitler's own portrait, and the other adorned with the swastika (Hakenkreuz), the emblem of the Nazi regime.

Kept in power with the help of the British and their exploitation of Iranian oil, Reza Shah was finally ousted from office in September 1941 by the British and their allies, who forced him into exile and installed his son, Mohammad Reza Pahlavi on the throne. Reza Shah's growing ties with Hitler prompted the British and Soviets to occupy parts of Iran. This military presence created lasting political problems for Iranians. The establishment of a one-party government in 1975 with the creation of the Rastakhiz Party systematically and institutionally

---

[2] French for "Memoirs of Tadj ol-Molouk", the wife of Reza Shah Pahlavi and the mother of Mohammad Reza Pahlavi.

eliminated political pluralism. This led to widespread civil discontent.

28 November – 1 December 1943 – Seated left to right: Joseph Stalin (Soviet Union), Franklin D. Roosevelt (United States), and Winston Churchill (United Kingdom) during the Tehran Conference, the first major summit of the Allied "Big Three" leaders during World War II. Held at the Soviet Embassy in Tehran, the meeting laid the groundwork for Operation Overlord (the D-Day invasion) and affirmed plans for postwar cooperation. (Photo: U.S. National Archives)

The hallmarks of Mohammad Reza Pahlavi's regime were autocracy and political repression. There was a lack of political freedom. The Shah wanted a mass organisation that would build up the "self-confidence and self-respect in the people, a belief in our power and ability…to fight the tendency of the people, especially the youth, to deny, to denigrate, to reject."[3] To patronize and disparage Iranian youth in this way was a serious error. Adding to the discontent, the Shah's secret police force, SAVAK, was notorious for its brutality, including widespread use of surveillance, censorship, torture, and assassination, to quash any kind of dissent. The Rastakhiz Party was not the first step toward autocracy, but among the final nails in the coffin of political freedom.

The Shah himself, speaking to a foreign reporter in 1973, exclaimed: "Your wonderful democracy. You'll see, in a few years, what your wonderful democracy leads to ... Freedom of thought, freedom of thought! Democracy, democracy! With five-year-olds going on strike and parading the streets. Is that what you call democracy? Freedom? ... Democracy, freedom, democracy! But what do these words mean?"[4]

---

[3] Ray Takeyh, "The Last Shah' America, Iran, and the fall of the Pahlavi Dynasty," Council of Foreign Relations Books, 26 January 2021. Available at: https://www.amazon.com/Last-Shah-America-Pahlavi-Relations/dp/030021779X

[4] Interview with Oriana Fallaci, published by the *New Republic* on 1 December 1973. Available at: https://newrepublic.com/article/92745/shah-iran-mohammad-reza-pahlevi-oriana-fallaci

16 January 1979 — The final departure of Shah Mohammad Reza Pahlavi and his wife Farah Diba from Iran amid escalating revolutionary tensions. They are seen walking across the tarmac at Mehrabad Airport as exiles took flight. (Photo: Pars News Agency)

The Shah initiated the so-called "White Revolution" in the 1960s, the major component of which was extensive land reforms that disrupted rural economies, dislocated millions of peasants, and intensified popular resentment. Despite being presented as progressive, these policies lacked genuine democratic intent and concentrated more power in the Shah's hands. The strategic aim of this policy was to curry favour with the Shah's main patron, the United States, which at the time provided him with substantial military support. Under the administration of President John F. Kennedy (1961–

1963), U.S. policy championed reforms in Iran, viewing them as a means to diminish the advent of a popular revolution against the monarchical dictatorship of the Shah.[5] These initiatives upended traditional social structures, often leaving the peasantry much worse off than before.

Ostensibly, the Shah claimed that he wanted to "modernize" Iran by adopting Western customs and behaviours, but many viewed his efforts as a profound erosion of Iranian identity and values, particularly in the rural heartlands. The agricultural sector, the lifeblood of the nation's economy, was all but obliterated by the Shah's reckless and poorly executed policies. What had been the foundation of Iran's economic stability was systematically dismantled, leaving the country's rural backbone in a state of ruin.

As a result, a wave of economically displaced rural inhabitants poured into the cities, overwhelming urban infrastructure that was woefully inadequate for such an influx. The desperate masses were relegated to sprawling suburban slums, where enormous shantytowns soon emerged as grim monuments to the unintended consequences of the Shah's mismanagement. In the end, the Shah's so-called

---

[5] Milani, Abbas. *The Shah*. Palgrave Macmillan, 2011. Available at:
https://abbasmilani.people.stanford.edu/publications/books/shah

'White Revolution' not only failed to modernize the country as promised but directly fuelled the rise of vast slums that, in later years, became hotbeds of discontent and prime recruiting grounds for Ayatollah Ruhollah Khomeini and the fundamentalist clerics.

6 March 1975 — Saddam Hussein and the Shah shaking hands at Algiers summit, where they signed the Algiers Agreement, settling the dispute over the Shatt al-Arab Waterway (Arvand Rud in Farsi). (Photo: Algerian Government Archive)

In the 1970s, Iran faced considerable economic problems, including soaring inflation and high unemployment, which sharply eroded living standards for ordinary Iranians.[6] The Shah's regime was also notorious for human rights abuses including curbing free speech, arbitrary arrests, and denying political freedoms. The combination of an economic downturn plus state oppression led inexorably to widespread public discontent.

Under the Shah's oppressive regime, the 1950s and 1960s were an era marked by severe repression against dissidents and political activists. The 1953 CIA- and MI6-orchestrated coup against Prime Minister Mohammad Mossadegh, who nationalized Iran's oil industry, deepened public resentment of Western meddling and helped cement the revolution's narrative of foreign domination. The Shah then forced all opposition groups and movements into silence and submission.[7] Through his brutal secret police, SAVAK, Pahlavi had established an iron-fisted rule.[8]

Although the Shah had support from Western countries, particularly the United States, this foreign backing became a source of resentment for many

---

[6] Katouzian, Homa. *The Political Economy of Modern Iran: Despotism and Pseudo-Modernism, 1926-1979*. Macmillan, 1981.
[7] Kinzer, Stephen. *All the Shah's Men: An American Coup and the Roots of Middle East Terror*. John Wiley & Sons, 2003.
[8] Amnesty International. "Report on Iran." Amnesty International Publications, 1975.

Iranians who saw the Shah as a puppet of Western interests. The global context of the Cold War also played a role, with regional instability and international power plays affecting Iran. Outwardly, Iran appeared to modernise rapidly, transitioning from a traditional, rural society to an industrial, urban one within a generation. However, the government's failure to deliver promised reforms, marred by corruption and incompetence, and more importantly, the SAVAK's brutal practices, sparked nationwide demonstrations in 1978.

Khomeini, who had done little, if anything, to oppose the Shah's oppressive policies while in exile in Najaf in Iraq, began to speak out against the Shah. He went to France in 1978, just as popular uprisings began in Iran. With his power-seeking instinct, he understood very well that the Shah had no future. But the problem was that the Shah and Saddam Hussein had met in Algiers in March 1975 and signed the famous Algiers Agreement, which resolved the differences between the two sides, and they had agreed, among other things, not to support each other's opposition. Therefore, with the escalation of the uprising in Iran in the second half of 1978, the Iraqi government and its intelligence service, which had maintained cordial relations with Khomeini and his entourage, respectfully asked him to either stop his activities against the Shah or leave Iraq. Khomeini moved to France in October 1978 and took advantage of the extensive media opportunities there, to gradually position himself as the leader of the opposition, by making hollow proclamations about civil liberties, equal rights for women, and promising to return to religious life in the mosque and not interfere in politics.

In those days, widespread protests, strikes, and demonstrations united various opposition groups ranging from secularists to communists to Islamists. All now demanded the overthrow of the monarchy. This unprecedented unity among diverse opposition groups facilitated the national revolutionary momentum. In January 1978, incensed by what they considered to be slanderous remarks made against Ayatollah Khomeini by the state-run newspaper Ettela'at, thousands took to the streets in the religious city of Qom. The Shah's police opened fire, killing nine demonstrators, though U.S. diplomats estimated the death toll to be at least fourteen.[9]

This was the beginning of a wave of popular uprisings across multiple cities, which forced the Shah to flee Iran a year later. The Shah, weakened by cancer and stunned by the sudden outpouring of hostility against him, wavered between limited concessions and violent repression. He wrongly attributed the protests to an international conspiracy. He relied heavily on Western advisers and representatives of the U.S. and

---

[9] Kurzman, Charles. "The Qum protests and the coming of the Iranian revolution, 1975 and 1978." *Social Science History* 27.3 (2003): 287-325.

UK, rather than seeking advice from his own ministers. Aware of growing frustration within the government ranks, Khomeini perceived that the Shah had lost his bearings and encouraged his followers to join the protests and take to the streets.

Scores of demonstrators were killed by government forces in the ensuing anti-regime protests, in a country where martyrdom played a very important spiritual role. Fatalities were followed by demonstrations to commemorate the customary 40-day milestone of mourning. Further casualties occurred at those protests, mortality and protest propelling one another forward. Thus, despite all government efforts, a cycle of violence began in which each death fuelled further protest, and all protest, from the secular left and religious right, was crowned by the rallying cry *Allāhu akbar* ("God is great"), heard at protests and issued from rooftops in the evenings. Gradually, the slogan "Death to the Shah" became the main slogan, and numerous songs and hymns were written for young people whose lives had been lost to the Shah's regime.

This series of escalating nationwide protests began to undermine and erode the power of the Shah's regime, which once appeared to wield absolute control over the country. The regime made limited concessions under mounting pressure of demonstrations, which demanded political freedoms and the release of political prisoners.

On 8 September 1978, the regime imposed martial law in more than 10 major cities, including Tehran, Isfahan, Shiraz, among others, and troops fired on demonstrators in Tehran, killing hundreds. Weeks later, government workers began to strike. On 31 October 1978, oil workers also went on strike, bringing the oil industry to a halt. Demonstrations continued to grow. On 10 December 1978, hundreds of thousands of protesters took to the streets in Tehran alone. The Shah's belated reform efforts failed to quell unrest. Rising unrest and a lack of genuine political engagement alienated the population further. Mounting pressures eventually forced the Shah to leave Iran on 16 January 1979. Ayatollah Khomeini returned from exile on 1 February 1979, subsequently leading to the final ousting of the monarchy and the establishment of the Islamic Republic of Iran.

1 February 1979 – Ruhollah Khomeini descends the steps of an Air France Boeing 747 at Mehrabad Airport, Tehran, returning from 15 years of exile in Iraq and France. (Photo: historydocuments.ir)

The overthrow of the monarchy in the 1979 revolution was widely seen by many Iranians as liberation from authoritarian rule. From the outset, Khomeini insisted that he and his clerical followers had always opposed the Shah and the monarchy and were thus entitled to claim a leadership role in his downfall. This narrative is contested by historians. The monarchy's relationship with the clergy, who hijacked the revolution to seize power, was a complex one. The Shah had initially shown fidelity to religious customs and leaned on the clergy during the first two decades of his rule. It was a symbiotic relationship.

The monarchy derived its legitimacy through religious sanction, and the clergy derived its social power and wealth from the monarchy's acquiescence. The two institutions were a major impediment to the formation of a developed civic society based on democratic values and human rights. The clergy, with the exception of a minority, tried to stay in the Shah's favour and maintained pervasive relations with SAVAK, the Shah's hated secret police, who brutally murdered and tortured political activists and intellectuals, including authors, academics, artists, and poets. But following widespread demonstrations against his oppressive rule, the Shah fled in January 1979 and did not return.

The overthrow of the Shah marked not only the end of a dynastic monarchy steeped in repression and excess, but also the beginning of a darker era that betrayed the hopes of the revolution. What began as a nationwide outcry for liberty, justice, and dignity was soon usurped by religious fundamentalists, plunging

Iran into a theocratic dictatorship far more brutal than the regime it replaced. While the Shah's authoritarianism drove many Iranians to despair, the subsequent rise of the Khomeini regime dismayed the people because many Iranians felt betrayed. The anti-Shah struggle evolved into resistance against the clerical regime. The ideals of the anti-monarchical revolution, namely democracy, justice, and the sovereignty of the people, have persisted to this day in the opposition to the theocratic regime, despite brutal repression, terrorism, and demonization.

16 January 1979 – A young man in Tehran holds aloft the Ettela'at headline "شاه رفت" ("The Shah has gone"), celebrating the Shah's departure from Iran, a turning point ushering in revolutionary transformation. (Photo: Ettela'at archives)

2

"Meet the new boss, same as the old boss."
— *Pete Townshend, The Who, "Won't Get Fooled Again"*

HOW AYATOLLAH RUHOLLAH KHOMEINI HIJACKED THE 1979 REVOLUTION

Cunning Ascent: Khomeini's Path to Power

According to the official narrative of the clerical regime, Khomeini was born in 1902 in Khomein city, in the central province of present-day Iran. Ruhollah Khomeini studied in a range of traditional Islamic seminaries and settled in the holy city of Qom around 1922, a city that is known as the intellectual centre of Shi'ite Islam. As a Shiite scholar and teacher, Khomeini wrote extensively on Islamic philosophy, law, and ethics.

Khomeini had no role in the political arena against Reza Shah. During the time of Mohammad Reza Shah, he was on the side of the coup against Dr. Mohammad Mossadegh, the popular prime minister of Iran, alongside reactionary mullahs such as his mentor Ayatollah Abolghassem Kashani. He remained politically obscure until the death of Ayatollah Seyyed Hossein Boroujerdi, the highest Shi'ite religious authority after the Second World War, in 1961. In 1962, after the White Revolution of the Shah, Khomeini emerged as an outspoken critic of the monarchy. Initially, in letters to the Shah, he asked him to reign in accordance with Islamic standards. But in the next steps, he sharpened his tone against the Shah, inspiring the riots that took place in late 1962 and the first half of 1963. He was arrested on June 5, 1963, after a fiery speech against the Shah at the Feyzieh School in Qom. Dozens of people were killed in the protests that took place in Tehran, Qom, and several other cities on that day.

21 July 1952 – Supporters of Prime Minister Mohammad Mossadegh flood the streets of Tehran, raising a large portrait of the nationalist leader during the height of Iran's oil nationalization movement and growing tension with the monarchy and foreign powers. (Photo: Pars News Agency)

Yet Khomeini was not advocating for freedom or democracy; he opposed the shah, among other reasons, because the regime had come under pressure to grant women the right to vote. Also, through his land reform policy, the Shah divided the lands belonging to landowners allied with the clerical establishment, thus destroying a significant part of their income. Moreover, his hostility to the monarchy was rooted in a deeply fundamentalist and reactionary interpretation of Islam.

To save Khomeini's life, a group of senior clerics in Qom and Najaf, including Ayatollahs Shariatmadari and Milani, declared Khomeini a *Marja'* (source of emulation). This initiative saved Khomeini's life. He was later and returned to Qom. Ironically, Ayatollah Shariatmadari, who was the initiator of this action, was subjected to the most severe pressure and repression 19 years later by the order of Khomeini, who had now come to power.

Another important development that took place in 1962 was that President Kennedy reached an understanding with the Shah. Kennedy, who became president in January 1961, wanted reforms in Iran and the premiership of people trusted by the United States, such as Ali Amini. The United States wanted to reduce the influence of Britain, and the feudal landowners left over from the past in the Shah's court. The Shah was worried that people like Amini would limit his power to the framework of the constitution.

During his visit to the United States in April 1962, the Shah promised President Kennedy that he would take the lead in reforms. Three months later, in August 1962, he gave the premiership to Asadollah Alam, a famous feudal lord in eastern Iran who was fully trusted by the Shah. In fact, the Shah and his court completed the turn they had made from Britain to the United States after the 1953 coup d'état. It was with such support that the Shah violently suppressed the uprisings of the first half of 1963, and especially the uprising of June 5, 1963. A year later, when Khomeini once again issued proclamations against the Shah, he was forcibly exiled from Iran to Turkey on November 5, 1964. Khomeini did not realize that the gap between the United States and the Shah had closed, unlike in 1962. Later, the Shah exiled him to the city of Najaf in Iraq, the country's religious counterpart to Qom in Iran. It was there that he began formulating his theories of *velāyat-e faqih* ("guardianship of the jurist") that would lay the foundations for the future Islamic republic in Iran.[10]

While in exile, Khomeini shrewdly built an influential network, positioning himself to assume the mantle of leadership in a popular movement for which he had paid no meaningful price. Behind the scenes, he quietly cultivated influence, ensuring that when the moment came, he could step in and claim ownership of a revolution that others had fought for.

During his exile in Iraq, Khomeini's opposition to the Shah was surprisingly muted. Far from being the firebrand revolutionary he later portrayed himself as, he made little effort to challenge the regime. In fact, at one point, he even remarked that his only desire was for the Shah to be "a good Shah", signalling a willingness to tolerate the monarchy under certain conditions.

---

[10] Khomeini, Ruhollah. *Islamic Government: Governance of the Jurist*. Manor Books, 1979.

Historical accounts, such as those by Abrahamian (1982),[11] suggest that some clerics maintained ties with SAVAK, sharing information to preserve their influence, though the extent of this collaboration remains debated. This covert collusion further casts doubt on Khomeini's revolutionary credentials. His transformation into the face of opposition seemed less about principle and more about seizing a political moment. Once the tides of public opinion turned decisively against the Shah, Khomeini opportunistically rebranded himself as the unwavering voice of resistance. In reality he was no stranger to the same political duplicity and self-preservation that characterized the regime he sought to replace.

Revolution Betrayed: Theocratic Tyranny Unleashed

As we have already seen, Khomeini left Iraq on 6 October 1978. Saddam Hussein's decision to expel Khomeini from Iraq in 1978 is often seen as a strategic miscalculation, which later contributed to the deep hostility between the two neighbouring nations, culminating in the Iran-Iraq War (1980-1988). Apart from being a close friend of the Shah, Saddam Hussein also feared Khomeini's influence over Iraq's Shi'ites, who make up 60 percent of the country's

---

[11] Abrahamian, Ervand. *Iran Between Two Revolutions.* Princeton University Press, 1982, pp. 473–80.

population and were dissatisfied with Saddam's predominantly Sunni Baathist dominance. After his expulsion from Iraq, Khomeini settled in Neauphle-le-Château, a suburb of Paris. From there, he positioned himself as an alternative to the Shah. His discourse resonated with many in a predominantly Muslim country disillusioned with Western influences.

The Shah had systematically eliminated or imprisoned Iran's secular and democratic opposition, while leaving the clerical establishment relatively untouched. In doing so, he created a fertile environment for the fundamentalist clerics to expand their organisational networks and spread their distorted ideology at a pivotal moment in the country's history. As opposition to the regime grew, the vacuum created by the repression of secular forces was quickly filled by the clergy and they became powerful political actors.

From his exile in France, Khomeini strategically leveraged these circumstances. He maintained lines of communication with his supporters inside Iran, using religious networks, particularly mosques largely left unregulated by the Shah's regime, to mobilize. Clerics became the primary channels through which Khomeini's messages were disseminated.

As documented by Milani (2008), Khomeini's cassette tapes were distributed through mosque networks and became the cornerstone of his propaganda.[12] Khomeini's supporters relayed his tape-recorded messages to an increasingly rebellious Iranian populace, and massive demonstrations, strikes, and civil unrest in late 1978 forced the departure of the Shah from Iran on 16 January 1979.

When Khomeini returned to Iran in triumph on 1 February 1979, after the Shah had fled, he was welcomed by several million people. Yet his return did not reflect a sustained or direct role in the revolutionary struggle against the regime but of calculated opportunism. By the time the public, frustrated with the Shah's oppressive policies, was ready to rally behind anyone who promised change, Khomeini stood poised to capitalize on their disillusionment, while true opponents were in prison. Declassified U.S. embassy cables from 1978 reveal American diplomats viewed him as a moderate religious figure who could stabilize Iran against Soviet influence. Naïvely believing that a new government led by an ostensibly religious figure would act as a buffer against communism and the Soviet Union, they tacitly facilitated Khomeini's rise to power, after receiving assurances from his western-educated emissaries that he would not dismantle the existing order, especially Iran's military.

---

[12] Milani, *op. cit.*

Ayatollah Khomeini's ability to hijack the 1979 Iranian Revolution was the result of strategic instrumentalization of Islamic doctrine, his ruthless opportunism, charismatic leadership, effective organisational skills, and adept manipulation of media and alliances. The suppression and imprisonment of democratic forces by the Shah and the chaotic conditions of the Pahlavi regime's final days gave Khomeini a unique opportunity to swiftly consolidate power as the old order crumbled. Western nations were caught off guard by the internal decay and sudden fall of the Iranian monarchy.

With the Shah's secular opposition imprisoned or silenced, and Western governments misjudging Khomeini's intentions, the vacuum of leadership was exploited to establish a theocracy that not only mirrored but often surpassed the despotism it replaced. Once in control, Khomeini swiftly moved to cement his regime under the doctrine of *velāyat-e faqih*, wielding absolute power over the state and silencing any form of opposition, including those who had risked everything to bring about the revolution.

Like most observers in the West, the Iranian people believed that this elderly, bearded, holy man, would restore peace, stability and prosperity to their nation. This hope was tragically misplaced. Little did they realise that Khomeini was a ruthless ideologue intent on plunging their country into a fundamentalist cauldron, exterminating anyone who stood in his way.

His corrupt system of *velāyat-e faqih* gave him the power to rule as Supreme Leader, claiming divine authority for every decision. He wielded this power with a calculated ferocity. Four days after his arrival in Iran, he announced the formation of a new government, and on 11 February 1979, senior Iranian military commanders declared their neutrality in the conflict between the government of Shapour Bakhtiar and the revolutionaries led by Khomeini. This effectively ended the Bakhtiar government and allowed Khomeini to seize the leadership.

After the Shah's ousting, Khomeini acted quickly and decisively to consolidate power. Through the establishment of the Islamic Revolutionary Guard Corps (IRGC) and revolutionary courts, as well as the drafting of an Islamic constitution, he marginalized and suppressed rival factions. He called for a national referendum, which resulted in the establishment of the Islamic Republic. His supporters effectively mobilized to secure a favourable outcome that solidified his vision for Iran's future. A national referendum in April showed overwhelming support for the institution of an Islamic republic, and the constitution of the new republic was approved in a referendum in December. Khomeini was named *"rahbar,"* Iran's political and religious leader for life.

Massoud Rajavi, who was released from prison four days after the Shah's escape, gained many supporters in a short period of time. In the first few months following the revolution, many young Iranians began to realize that Khomeini had deceived them. Many of them were attracted to the PMOI and its leader, Massoud Rajavi, who was barred from the presidential race for refusing to endorse the new constitution or the principle of *velãyat-e faqih*.

In 1981, when Khomeini deposed President Abolhassan Banisadr, and a new wave of arrests and executions began in the country, Massoud Rajavi and Banisadr left Tehran's main military air base for Paris in an incredible getaway operation, piloted by the best pilot of the Iranian Air Force, Behzad Moezzi. Moezzi, once the Shah's trusted pilot, had secretly joined the Mojahedin. Earlier, Rajavi had announced the formation National Council of Resistance of Iran (NCRI) with the aim of replacing the Khomeini regime with a democratic republic in Tehran. His presence in Paris was an opportunity to introduce this congress to the world.

Massoud Rajavi and pilot Colonel Behzad Moezzi, 1981. (Photo: NCRI).

Khomeini began pressuring the French government to expel Massoud Rajavi from France or to stop his political activities. President François Mitterrand and his socialist government gave in less to these pressures. But, with the election to the French parliament and the victory of the centre-right Rally for the Republic (RPR) party, Jacques Chirac became prime minister. The regime seized the opportunity to open a deal with the new government over the release of French hostages in Lebanon. The pressure on the PMOI and Rajavi began. Ultimately, Rajavi and around 1,000 members of the PMOI left Paris for Iraq in June 1986. The PMOI established bases near the Iranian border, the largest of which was Camp Ashraf in the northeast province of Diyala.

Meanwhile, Khomeini himself proved unwavering in his determination to transform Iran into a theocratically ruled Islamic state. Iran's Shi'ite clerics largely took over the formulation of governmental policy, while Khomeini arbitrated between the various revolutionary factions and made final decisions on important matters requiring his personal authority. As Supreme Leader, Khomeini first executed the former top generals and officials of the Shah. Then the remaining domestic opposition was crushed, its members being systematically imprisoned or executed. Iranian women were forced to wear the veil, Western music and alcohol were banned, and corporal and capital punishments drawn from strict interpretations of Sharia law were reinstated.

The main focus of Khomeini's foreign policy was to confront the United States. In addition, Iran tried to export its brand of Islamic fundamentalism to neighbouring Muslim countries, especially among their Shi'ite populations. Iraq, with its majority Shi'ite population, its long borders with Iran and the Imam Ali Mosque in Najaf – a holy shrine for Shi'ites, held particular strategic and religious significance.

On 4 November 1979, the U.S. Embassy in Tehran was occupied by students close to Khomeini and American diplomatic personnel were held hostage for 444 days. Khomeini hailed the seizure of the embassy as a 'Second Revolution', using it to galvanize anti-

American sentiment. He also refused to support a peaceful solution to the Iran-Iraq war, which began in 1980 and which he insisted on prolonging in the hope of toppling Saddam. Finally, in 1988, after years of bloodshed and the growing threat posed by the National Liberation Army and the Mojahedin, Khomeini accepted the cease-fire as a poisoned chalice.

Four decades later, the legacy of Khomeini's hijacking of the revolution is stark. Iran became a bastion of clerical authoritarianism, supporting extremist proxy groups abroad, suppressing internal dissent, marginalising women, prolonging the war, and presiding over economic collapse. The promise of democracy, justice, and freedom that animated millions of Iranians in 1979 was betrayed by a regime that cloaked its brutality in religious garb. Yet, the resilience of the Iranian people endures, and the vision of freedom lives on in the democratic resistance movements that continue to challenge the regime's authority. History may well remember Khomeini not as a liberator, but as a vicious tyrant cloaked in piety.

3

"Religious tyranny differs in no way from political tyranny."
— *John Adams*

VELĀYAT-E FAQIH – A TOXIC PHILOSOPHY

Clerical Tyranny: The Grip of Velāyat-e faqih

Velāyat-e faqih ("guardianship of the Islamic jurist") is a doctrine that grants ultimate political and religious authority to a senior cleric, purportedly acting under divine mandate. Championed and institutionalized by Khomeini, it became the foundational principle of governance in the Islamic Republic of Iran following the 1979 revolution.

Susan B. Anthony[13], the American social reformer, women's rights activist and pioneer of the women's

---

[13] Susan B. Anthony - *The North American Review*, Vol. 175, No. 553 (Dec. 1902), pp. 800-810. Available at:
https://www.jstor.org/stable/i25150951

suffrage movement in the U.S. said: *"I distrust people who know so well what God wants them to do, because I notice it always coincides with their own desires."* This insight aptly captures the nature of Iran's theocratic regime, where the doctrine of velāyat-e faqih or absolute clerical guardianship provides ideological justification for authoritarian practices, including public executions, suppression of dissent, and systemic human rights abuses, all cloaked in claims of divine authority.

For more than four decades, since Khomeini came to power, the clerical regime has ruled Iran with an iron fist, suppressing freedom and justice, violating human rights and women's rights, and ordering assassinations. From the very beginning of its establishment, the regime in Tehran was based on the dual pillars of internal subjugation and the export of terrorism and reactionary religious beliefs. The policy of exporting Islamic fundamentalism and extremism has been a cornerstone of state strategy, contained within the Iranian regime's constitution since its foundation.

While *velāyat-e faqih* centralizes power in the Supreme Leader, elected institutions like the parliament and presidency exist, though their authority is heavily constrained by the Guardian Council, appointed by the Supreme Leader, effectively eliminating democratic governance and political pluralism. Dissent is often met with arrest, imprisonment, or worse. The regime has been accused of numerous human rights abuses, including suppression of free speech, arbitrary detention, systemic discrimination against minorities, and lack of due process. Human rights organisations frequently report on these violations, further fuelling domestic and international criticism.

A look at the constitution of the religious dictatorship makes the nature and structure of this regime very clear:

Exporting the Revolution

The preamble to the constitution states: "In the formation and equipping of the country's defence forces, attention is paid to faith and doctrine as the basis and criterion. Therefore, the Army of the Islamic Republic of Iran and the Revolutionary Guards Corps will be formed in accordance with the above goal and will not only protect and protect the borders but will also be responsible for the mission of the school of thought, i.e., jihad for the sake of God and the struggle for the spread of the rule of God's law in the world.

In Article 3 of the Constitution, two of the duties of the Islamic Republic are stated as follows: Adjusting the country's foreign policy based on the criteria of Islam, fraternal commitment to all Muslims, and unwavering support for the oppressed of the world.

Article 11 of the Constitution: According to the Qur'an, all Muslims are one Ummah and the government of the Islamic Republic of Iran is obliged to base its general policy on the alliance and unity of Islamic nations and make consistent efforts to realize the political, economic and cultural unity of the Islamic world.

Article 91: In order to safeguard the provisions of Islam and the Constitution in terms of the non-contradiction of the decisions of the Islamic Consultative Assembly with them, a council called the Guardian Council shall be formed with the following composition:

1. Six just jurists who are aware of the requirements of the time and the issues of the day. The choice of these people is with the Supreme Leader.

2. Six jurists, in various fields of law, from among Muslim jurists who are introduced to the Islamic Consultative Assembly by the Head of the Judiciary and elected by the vote of the Parliament. (The head of the judiciary is elected by the Supreme Leader and the members of the parliament are filtered by the same Guardian Council.

Article 110 Duties and Powers of the Leader:

1. Determining the general policies of the Islamic Republic of Iran after consultation with the Expediency Council.
2. Supervising the proper implementation of the general policies of the system
3. The Referendum Order
4. Commander-in-Chief of the Armed Forces
5. Declaring war and peace and mobilizing forces
6. Appointment, dismissal, and acceptance of resignation: (a) Jurists of the Guardian Council (b) The highest official of the Judiciary (c) Head of the Islamic Republic of Iran Broadcasting Organization (d) Chairman of the Joint Chiefs of Staff, Commander-in-Chief of the Islamic Revolutionary Guard Corps (IRGC) (e) Supreme Commanders of Military and Police Forces
7. Resolving disputes and regulating the relations between the three branches
8. Solving the problems of the system, which cannot be solved by ordinary means, through the Expediency Council.
9. Signing the Presidential Decree after the People's Election – The qualifications of presidential candidates, in terms of meeting the conditions stipulated in this law, must be approved by the Guardian Council before the election and approved by the Supreme Leader in the first term.
10. Dismissal of the President, taking into account the interests of the country, after the Supreme Court's

ruling that he has violated his legal duties, or the Islamic Consultative Assembly's vote on his incompetence based on Article 89.

11. Pardoning or commuting the sentences of convicts within the limits of Islamic standards after the recommendation of the Head of the Judiciary.

This concentration of power in the hands of the Supreme Leader, while there is no control or monitoring mechanism over it, clearly shows the dimensions of this absolute dictatorship. On the other hand, it shows how vulgar the electoral mechanisms in this regime are.

Beyond the Constitution this system imposes strict social rules based on a dogmatic and distorted interpretation of Islamic law, affecting everything from dress codes to personal behaviours. There is a significant cultural and generational gap in Iran. The rigid rules imposed by the *velãyat-e faqih* often clash with the more liberal attitudes of the younger generation, who make up a large portion of the population. Many young Iranians find these restrictions incompatible with their aspirations for personal freedoms and modern lifestyles.

There are approximately 45 million women in the Islamic Republic of Iran, over half under the age of thirty.[14] Women make up more than 50% of university students, but, because of misogyny and blatant discrimination creating obstacles to employment, they account for only around 19% of Iran's workforce.[15] At a time when women in many parts of the world have achieved political, economic, personal and social equality, Iranian women are amongst the most repressed globally, ruled by a regime dominated by elderly, misogynist clerics.

But young Iranian women are becoming increasingly engaged in the growing opposition movement.[16] In the repeated nationwide uprisings, tens of thousands of courageous female teachers, medical staff, students, factory workers and pensioners have taken to the streets to demand an end to corruption, an end to discrimination, and repression as well as an end to the regime's aggressive military adventurism across the Middle East. Following the death in custody of the young Kurdish woman Mahsa Amini and the nationwide uprising that followed in 2022, women who led the protests gained international recognition. The slogan "Women, Resistance, Freedom" which has

---

[14] World Bank data as of 2023. Available at:
https://data.worldbank.org/indicator/SP.POP.TOTL.FE.IN?end=2023&locations=IR&start=1960&view=chart
[15] U.S. State Department, "2021 Country Reports on Human Rights Practices: Iran". Available at:
https://www.state.gov/reports/2021-country-reports-on-human-rights-practices/iran
[16] NCRI Women Committee, "December 2023 Report: Iranian Women Remain Resilient", 31 December 2023.
https://wncri.org/2023/12/31/december-2023-report/

been echoed by women political prisoners has gained popularity in Iranian prisons.

The theocratic dictatorship in Iran has a history of targeting women with oppressive laws that would not be tolerated in the West or indeed in most civilized countries. In Iran women are considered the legal property of their closest male relative. Girls as young as nine can be married off by their parents.[17] A woman's testimony in court is worth only half that of a man's.[18] Women may not seek to have a man charged with rape unless they have four independent witnesses.[19] All family relationships are strictly controlled by Sharia law.

Women's dress codes are also under constant scrutiny. They must wear the hijab and 'morality police' are on relentless patrol to enforce the law. Women, particularly young women, are singled out for brutal attacks for the 'crime' of mal veiling.[20] Girls

---

[17] Civil Code of the Islamic Republic of Iran, Article 1041. Available at: https://faolex.fao.org/docs/pdf/ira206827.pdf
[18] Islamic Penal Code of the Islamic Republic of Iran, Articles 199 and 209. Available at:
https://sherloc.unodc.org/cld/uploads/res/islamic-penal-code_html/Islamic_Penal_Code.pdf
[19] U.S. State Department, "2019 Country Reports on Human Rights Practices: Iran". Available at:
https://www.state.gov/reports/2019-country-reports-on-human-rights-practices/iran/
[20] Amnesty International, "Pro-government vigilantes attack women for standing up against forced hijab laws", 12 May 2019. Available at: https://www.amnesty.org/en/latest/press-

who were deemed to be improperly dressed in the street have suffered horrific acid attacks and stabbings, in assaults openly condoned by the mullahs.[21] Teenage girls and women, arrested for the offence of posting videos of themselves dancing or singing on social media, have been publicly flogged.[22] Young female students attending end-of-term parties have been fined and beaten. This is what gender equality looks like in Iran today.

Khomeini stated that equality between women and men contradicted Islam and defied the Quran. One of his first acts after taking power was to abolish the 'Family Protection Law' that gave women family rights. He also cancelled social services for women and abolished the role of female judges in Iran's justice system. Today, only 6% of MPs in Iran are women.[23]

---

release/2019/03/iran-pro-government-vigilantes-attack-women-for-standing-up-against-forced-hijab-laws/
[21] Saeed Kamali Dehghan, "Iranian journalists detained after reporting on acid attacks", 28 October 2014. Available at: https://www.theguardian.com/world/iran-blog/2014/oct/28/iranian-journalists-detained-reporting-acid-attacks
[22] "Iranian Woman Defiant Despite 'Medieval' Flogging For Hijab Violation", Radio Free Europe, 9 January 2024. Available at: https://www.rferl.org/a/iran-women-defiant-flogging-hijab-violation/32767635.html
[23] State-run Hamshahri daily (Persian), 27 May 2020. Available at: https://hamshahrionline.ir/news/515463/-زن-۱۶-اینفوگرافیک
تعداد-مقایسه-نگاه-یک-در-یازدهم-مجلس-نماینده

Defiant Hope: Resisting for a Democratic Iran

And yet Iranian women are at the forefront of the resistance to the theocratic dictatorship. Indeed, the main democratic opposition movement, the National Council of Resistance of Iran (NCRI) is led by a woman, Maryam Rajavi.[24] Brave women are now routinely joining their brothers to demand regime change and an end to the misogyny and repression which has terrorized not only the Iranian people for the past four decades, but a vast part of the Middle East as well.

The ideological focus of the regime undermines effective economic governance. Misallocation of resources to fund proxy groups and military ventures abroad rather than investing in domestic development has led to economic collapse and high unemployment, with disproportionate impact on Iran's young labour force.

Corruption within the political elite has also been an entrenched feature of governance. Power is often concentrated among a small group of clerics and their allies, creating an environment where corruption can thrive. This erodes public trust and exacerbates frustration with the system. The ideological stance of the *velāyat-e faqih* regime has precipitated punitive

---

[24] Maryam Rajavi's Biography, National Council of Resistance of Iran. Available at: https://www.ncr-iran.org/en/maryam-rajavi/

international sanctions and heightened Iran's diplomatic isolation. This has adversely affected the Iranian economy and the everyday lives of its citizens, further contributing to the general discontent.

Iran's Supreme Leader presides over a systemic corruption, at the centre of which is the sinister Islamic Revolutionary Guard Corps (IRGC), the regime's repressive security apparatus, which answers directly to the Supreme Leader and dominates key sectors including construction, energy, telecommunications, and banking. The IRGC pays no taxes and diverts national wealth into elite patronage networks, while sponsoring terrorism and aggressive military expansionism abroad. The IRGC runs construction companies and missile factories and is largely responsible for the regime's ongoing nuclear programme, which never ceased, despite President Barack Obama's Joint Comprehensive Plan of Action (JCPOA) flawed nuclear deal. Khomeini created the IRGC and its extra-territorial Quds Force to spread his revolutionary policy of violence and terror beyond Iran's borders.

The IRGC and its Quds Force not only brutally enforces the clerical regime's oppressive domination of Iran's population, but it also spreads its terror network worldwide. The implementation of a grossly distorted version of Sharia law, under the diktat of the misogynist mullahs, soon saw the role of women reduced to that of second-class citizens, while Iran's judicial system became one of the most brutal in the world.

The Iranian regime executes more people per capita than any other country. It carries out more total executions than any nation but China, whose population is over 17 times greater than that of Iran.[25] Tehran continues to target political dissidents and ethnic, religious, and sexual minorities for execution. Capital punishment can be—and often is—carried out against juvenile offenders and for nonviolent crimes.

The current Supreme Leader, Ayatollah Ali Khamenei, followed the homicidal example set by his predecessor Ruhollah Khomeini, appointing Ebrahim Raisi – 'The Butcher of Tehran' as president in 2021 to consolidate power within his own faction and unify his regime against the growing waves of nationwide unrest. During Raisi's tenure, the rate of executions increased exponentially in tandem with further repression against ordinary citizens. Moreover, the regime resorted to carrying out brutal punishments in public in the hope of causing widespread fear, thus preventing future protests.

Over the past four decades, the regime has employed widespread use of barbaric acts such as amputation of hands and feet, gouging eyes, stoning people to death,

---

[25] Amnesty International, "Death sentences and executions in 2023", 29 May 2024. Available at:
https://www.amnesty.org/en/documents/act50/7952/2024/en/

throwing prisoners off cliffs, and other brutal punishments. As a prosecutor in Hamedan in the 1980s, Ebrahim Raisi enforced harsh penalties under the regime's judicial system.[26]

The cruelty and inhumanity of Iran's judicial system goes well beyond executions, however. Individuals may be arrested and indefinitely detained without charge or on trumped-up offenses, subject to degrading treatment, including torture in order to extract confessions. They are denied rights such as access to legal counsel and a fair and speedy trial, and sentenced to other barbaric penalties such as amputation, blinding, and flogging. Amnesty International reported Iran accounted for 72% of global executions in 2022–2023.[27] The regime amputates fingers of those charged with theft, a brutal punishment under its penal code.[28]

Those accused or convicted of perpetrating crimes are incarcerated in overcrowded prisons where they may be subject to torture, rape, and other atrocities. Iran's overcrowded and unsanitary penitentiaries are also

---

[26] Amnesty International. Iran: Presidency of Ebrahim Raisi a Grim Reminder of the Crisis of Impunity. June 19, 2021, www.amnesty.org/en/documents/mde13/4314/2021/en/
[27] Amnesty International. Death Sentences and Executions 2023. Amnesty International, 2024; Amnesty International. *Death Sentences and Executions 2022*. Amnesty International, 2023.
[28] Amnesty International. "Iranian Officials Must Be Held Accountable for Amputating the Fingers of Two Men." Amnesty International, July 29, 2022.

breeding grounds for the coronavirus, flu and other illnesses, and prisoners are often denied necessary medical care, personal protective equipment, and disinfectant. Iran executes the majority of convicts sentenced to death by hanging within these prisons. The regime, however, also sometimes carries out executions in public. Public hanging from cranes is a method designed to instil fear through spectacle and prolong suffering.

Following the sudden and unexpected death of Ebrahim Raisi in a helicopter accident on 19 May 2024, the Islamic republic was thrown into a state of confusion. Raisi had been a figure deeply implicated in systemic political executions. He played a key role as a member of the 'death commission' in Tehran, during the 1988 massacre of more than 30,000 political prisoners, mostly supporters or members of the opposition PMOI. While the ultimate head of state in Iran is the unelected Supreme Leader, the president is the second most powerful, but with significantly less authority.

The mullahs organized a hasty presidential election to find a replacement for Raisi. Of the 80 registered candidates, only six were approved—each with absolute fealty to Khamenei. The electoral process was widely regarded as stage-managed, with candidates publicly pledging allegiance to the Supreme Leader.

The election of Masoud Pezeshkian as Iran's supposedly "reformist" president in July 2024 quickly began with an unprecedented tsunami of executions. The number of executions has reached over 1,400 since Pezeshkian became president in August 2024. Many of those hanged were sentenced to death for "waging war against God".

The IRGC's involvement in proxy wars throughout the Middle East has caused outrage across Iran, where the economy has collapsed, the rial is in freefall and 75% of the population now struggle to survive on incomes that have fallen below the international poverty line. Iranians are appalled that their money has been stolen by the mullahs to finance the IRGC and its involvement for decades in backing the now-disposed Bashar al-Assad's bloody civil war in Syria, the Houthi rebels in Yemen, the brutal Shi'ite militias in Iraq, the terrorist Hezbollah in Lebanon and Hamas in Gaza.

The fall of Assad and the effective decapitation of Hezbollah and Hamas and the pummelling of the Houthis by the Americans, have fundamentally changed the situation and severely weakened the Iranian regime. But if the opportunity arises, the regime will try to rebuild its evil network in the region, some of which activity has already started.

Iran's nearly 90 million population view the *velãyat-e faqih* system as toxic. While a small percentage of the population, four percent[29] according to the Parliament Speaker Mohammad Bagher Ghalibaf, remain loyal to the ideology, a growing number of Iranians, particularly among the youth, seek the overthrow of the mullahs' theocratic regime and the introduction of an entirely new system in a secular republic, that better aligns with their aspirations for freedom, justice, and economic prosperity.

Fundamentalist groups, including Sunni groups such as ISIS, Al-Qaeda, the Taliban, Boko Haram, Al-Shabaab, and Shi'ite groups such as Hezbollah, Ansar al-Islam, the Iraqi popular mobilization force (PMF) militias, etc., as well as dozens of other groups, who fight each other like cats in a sack, nevertheless all look to Tehran as the core of Islamic fundamentalism. That is why regime change in Tehran will sound the death-knell for these extremist Islamist groups around the world. It is time the West woke up to the fact that as long as the mullahs remain in power there will be no possibility of peace in the Middle East. The mullahs will always be the problem. They can never be part of the solution.

The regime's brutality has not only undermined Iran's economic and social fabric but has destabilised the entire Middle East, turning Iran into a pariah state,

---

[29] "Ghalibaf and his 96% movement," state-run Bahar newspaper, May 2, 2017 (in Farsi).
https://www.pishkhan.com/news/14767

feared by its neighbours and distrusted by its own people.

And yet, as the regime doubles down on its repression, the will of the Iranian people to reclaim their future continues to grow stronger. Young Iranians, led increasingly by women, are confronting the regime with courage and clarity. They demand a future free from clerical domination, where democracy, human dignity, and equality are not hollow promises but lived realities. The growing call for regime change and the dismantling of the *velāyat-e faqih* system is not a cry for revenge, but a declaration of hope—a call for a secular, democratic republic where governance is based not on divine claims, but on the sovereign will of the people.

4

"In war, truth is the first casualty."
— *Aeschylus*

THE WAR WITH IRAQ

Provoking Chaos: Khomeini's Warpath Ignited

Ayatollah Ruhollah Khomeini's enmity with Saddam Hussein has deep roots that predate the 1979 Iranian Revolution, tracing back to the 1960s and 1970s during Khomeini's exile in Iraq. Saddam Hussein had normalized relations with the Shah under the 1975 Algiers Agreement. In 1978, when Khomeini began issuing proclamations and speeches against the Shah, Saddam pressured him to exercise restraint or leave Iraq. Saddam, like the leaders of the great powers at that time, did not think that the Shah would be so politically vulnerable and would soon be overthrown, otherwise he would certainly not have made such a request. By all accounts, Khomeini left Iraq on 6 October 1978, and settled in Neauphle-le-Château, a suburb of Paris. Khomeini harboured lasting resentment toward Saddam for this perceived betrayal.

From the first months of his rule, Khomeini declared his intention to "export the revolution" to Iraq. He explicitly declared that his next goal was to create an "Islamic State" in Baghdad. His rhetoric, which rejected geographical limitations to the cause of Islamic fundamentalism, unnerved neighbouring countries, particularly Iraq.

Ayatollah Hossein Ali Montazeri, Khomeini's designated successor at the time, later wrote: "In the context of foreign policy, slogans were based on exporting the revolution, and the revolution recognizes no geographical borders. These slogans made neighbouring countries very nervous."

Iraq possessed unique political, geopolitical, economic, and religious characteristics. At least 60 percent of the Shi'ite population, 1,200 kilometres of common borders, and the presence of the tombs of six Shi'ite Imams in Karbala, Najaf, Baghdad, and Samarra. Iraq also possesses vast oil reserves. More importantly, dominating Iraq would have granted the Iranian regime strategic access to the land borders of Kuwait, Saudi Arabia, Jordan, and Syria, while significantly reducing its geographical distance to Israel by 700 to 800 kilometres.

From the very beginning, Khomeini calculated that the hostility between the Iraqi government and the government of Hafez al-Assad in Syria, and his strategic calculation was that by dominating Iraq, he would have a way to the Mediterranean coast, the land borders of Israel and Lebanon. Especially since Lebanon, where a third of the population was Shi'ite, was a good platform for the regime. Lebanon, with a sizable Shi'ite population and longstanding religious-cultural ties to Iran dating back to the Safavid era (one of Iran's most significant ruling dynasties reigning from 1501 to 1736), was seen as an ideal staging ground for regional influence.

These calculations made Iraq extremely valuable to Khomeini. But Khomeini knew very well that the invasion of Iraq and the occupation of this country would turn against him, and the world would not accept such an act of aggression, in addition to lacking the military capacity for direct intervention. Khomeini invested in exporting the revolution and inciting the Iraqi people and army against the Ba'athist regime.

In the months leading up to the outbreak of war, Tehran's rhetoric became increasingly incendiary. Five months before hostilities began, Iranian newspapers openly urged for the Iraqi army to rebel against Saddam Hussein, with headlines proclaiming, "Imam [Khomeini] encourages the Iraqi army to rise up and revolt."30 This verbal provocation was followed by direct actions. For example, in April 1980, Iraq's deputy prime minister, Tariq Aziz, narrowly escaped an assassination attempt orchestrated by Iranian-backed operatives.31 These provocations heightened tensions.

In the meantime, Saddam Hussein suggested to Khomeini through intermediaries that the problems between them should be resolved through dialogue and announced his readiness to travel to Iran himself and meet with Khomeini directly. But Khomeini, who wanted to overthrow Saddam, rejected this proposal sharply.

Iran's Foreign Ministry convened regular strategy sessions, with particular focus on Iraq. Senior diplomats, including Iran's ambassador to Baghdad, attended to formulate key policy directives aimed at destabilizing Saddam's regime."32

Almost five months before the start of the war, Hossein Ali Montazeri, Khomeini's nominated successor at the time, urged Khomeini to extend his leadership to the burgeoning Iraqi opposition. In a

---

[30] State-run *Kayhan* daily, 19 April 1980.
[31] "Christian outsider in Saddam's inner circle," *The Guardian*, 25 April 2003. Available at
https://www.theguardian.com/world/2003/apr/25/iraq.brianwhitaker
[32] State-run daily, Kayhan, 27 October 1979, 18 December 2001.

meeting with Khomeini, he said: "These days, our Iraqi brothers regularly come and say that just as Imam Khomeini led the Iranian revolution to fruition, we expect them to lead the Iraqi revolution as well."[33]

The newspaper affiliated with the ruling Islamic Republic Party frequently published articles promoting the concept of an 'Islamic Revolution' in Iraq and advocating for its occupation and conquest. Once, on September 9, 1980, less than two weeks before the Iraqi army's invasion of Iran, he wrote: "By the order of the Imam, the Commander-in-Chief of the Armed Forces, the revolutionary forces announced their readiness to occupy Iraq with the support of Muslims."

---

[33] Bamdad newspaper, 15 April 15, 1970, and 4 July 2001.

Kayhan newspaper, 9 April 1980, Headline reads, "Imam called on Iraqi Army to revolt. (Photo: Kayhan newspaper)

Against this backdrop of escalating rhetoric and provocations, Iraq launched a pre-emptive invasion of Iran's western provinces on 22 September 1980. In fact, Saddam Hussein fell into the trap that Khomeini had set for him. Saddam mollified the 1975 Algiers Agreement, which had previously settled territorial disputes in Iran's favour, and declared that Iraq was no longer bound by its provisions.

Prolonged Agony: Devastation and Dissent Crushed

"On paper, Saddam's armed forces were stronger, with an army of 200,000 troops equipped with 2,850 tanks. His air force stood at 38,000 personnel with

332 combat aircraft. The Iranian army had 150,000 men with 2,000 tanks and an air force of 70,000 with 445 combat aircraft. Although the Iraqi navy was negligible, Iran had 20,000 naval personnel with a fleet of a dozen destroyers, frigates, and corvettes. While Saddam's forces were largely equipped with Soviet-supplied weapons, Iran's forces had British and American equipment that would eventually run out of spares. Saddam also counted on many Iranian units being in disarray as a result of the revolution."[34]

Despite the occupation of parts of Iran's territory with his authoritarian regime, Khomeini understood very well that the war would end in favour of consolidating his power, silencing or suppressing internal dissent would become more legitimate, the power of mobilizing the people in the name of defending the homeland would be easier, and the possibility of strengthening the Revolutionary Guards, which was his private army, would be more powerful against the classic army left over from the time of the Shah. He mentioned the title of divine gift.

The PMOI, along with other dissident forces, were swiftly branded as "fifth columnists".[35] This labelling

---

[34] *The Guardian, op. cit.*
[35] When Iraqi forces attacked Iranian territory, the PMOI issued a statement on 23 October 1980, condemning the Iraqi action They also rushed to Khuzestan province to fight against Iraqi forces. Several PMOI members, including Dr. Ahmad Tabatabai, were killed at the war fronts and many were captured. *Mojahed*, Special Issue, 1 November 1980.

provided the regime with the justification to brutally suppress any form of dissent. This was despite the fact that the PMOI strongly condemned the occupation of Iranian territory by the Iraqi army from the beginning, and many of its members and supporters participated in the war fronts against Iraq. Some of them were captured and released 10 years later, some were killed at the front, and some were targeted by the Revolutionary Guards.

By May 1982, however, the dynamics of the war shifted. Iraqi forces withdrew from all Iranian territory, retreating to internationally recognised borders, and Saddam Hussein sought a ceasefire. However, Khomeini, who had been able to expel the Iraqi forces from Iranian territory, strongly opposed the ceasefire and peace, emphasizing that peace would cause the burial of Islam, and with the slogan of conquering Quds through Karbala, he sought to occupy Iraqi territory, especially the strategic city of Basra. Thus, an illegitimate war continued for six years, killing hundreds of thousands of people in Iran and hundreds of thousands in Iraq. Ali Akbar Hashemi Rafsanjani, then Speaker of Parliament and Khomeini's de facto deputy, later lamented that the war had cost Iran over $1 trillion in damages.

Domestic and international calls for the end of the war were increasing every day. In January 1983, Iraqi Deputy Prime Minister Tariq Aziz met with Massoud Rajavi, President of the NCRI, in Auvers-sur-Oise near Paris. They issued a joint declaration asserting that the ongoing war was not the will of the Iranian people, but rather the ideological war of the Khomeini regime.

Subsequently, on 13 March 1983, the NCRI unanimously adopted a seven-point peace plan that prioritized Iran's national interests. Especially since the basis of peace was the 1975 Algiers Agreement, which was entirely in favour of Iran and was torn apart by Saddam Hussein. The agreement was accepted by the Iraqi government as an acceptable basis for peace. The plan garnered international endorsement from over 5,000 political figures, including government ministers, party leaders, and members of parliament.

The United Nations Security Council passed several resolutions calling for a ceasefire between Iraq and Iran. However, Khomeini categorically rejected both international and domestic calls for peace, continuing to promote the slogan 'liberate Qods [Jerusalem] via Karbala' as justification for extending the war.

The decision to prolong the war for six years, despite the Iraqi withdrawal and offers of peace, came at an immense cost to the Iranian people. One of the regime's former IRGC commanders candidly admitted, "If the war didn't take place, I think the

Islamic Republic would have collapsed... That is how we were able to clamp down on the grouplets."[36]

Child soldiers in the Iran Iraq War 1980-1988 (Photo: Iranwire.com)

In contrast to the beginning of the war, which had a popular legitimacy, and many volunteers went to the war fronts, this legitimacy became less and less after the withdrawal of Iraqi forces from Iranian territory. In a way, despite the fact that Iran's population was three times that of Iraq, it faced serious problems in the war mobilization. Desertion from the fronts had become commonplace, and successive blows on the fronts forced Khomeini to accept a ceasefire.

---

[36] Javad Mansouri, interview with state-run TV, 7 October 2017. Available at: https://vimeo.com/420325567

The human and economic toll was staggering. Khomeini, who likened accepting the ceasefire to 'drinking a chalice of poison,' had prolonged a conflict that resulted in over one million Iranian deaths and more than $1 trillion in damages.[37] Survivors like Ahmad, a teenage conscript, recalled, 'We were sent into minefields with plastic keys to paradise, promised martyrdom.'[38]

Former Iranian President Ali Akbar Hashemi Rafsanjani later admitted that the war had left Iran devastated, with over 50 cities and 3,000 villages destroyed and millions displaced. These losses were not inevitable; they were the direct consequence of Khomeini's ideological intransigence and refusal to accept peace.

The retrospective critiques from within the regime further underscore Khomeini's role in prolonging the conflict. Montazeri's 1987 letters to Khomeini, later published in his memoirs (2001),[39] sharply criticized the continuation of the war as unjust and contrary to Islamic principles.[40] Mohsen Rezai, a former IRGC commander-in-chief, admitted in 2016 that "Iranian

---

[37] Rafsanjani, Tehran Friday Prayers' sermon, 9 August 1991.
[38] BBC Interview, 2010
[39] Khaterāt-e Āyatollāh Montazeri, Memoirs of Ayatollah Montazeri), published in multiple volumes by the Office of Grand Ayatollah Montazeri in Qom, 2001.
[40] National Security Archive. (September 20, 2021). Ayatollah Hossein Ali Montazeri, Letter to Ayatollah Ruhollah Khomeini, 7 October 1985.

forces should not have entered Iraqi territory" once Iraq had retreated. 41 These admissions reveal that inside Iran public opinion was deeply hostile to the regime's disastrous and unpatriotic decisions during the war, forcing many even within the regime, to criticize the nature of the war's extension in recent years.

The Iran-Iraq War was not an inevitable consequence of regional geopolitics; rather, it was a conflict deliberately inflamed and prolonged by the ideological zealotry and expansionist ambitions of Ayatollah Khomeini. Had Iran been governed by a conventional state apparatus focused on national sovereignty and diplomacy, rather than by a theocracy bent on exporting Islamic extremism, the provocations that prompted Saddam Hussein's pre-emptive invasion might never have occurred.

Ultimately, the war devastated Iran's economy, claimed the lives of over a million people, and entrenched the clerical regime's authoritarian grip on power. The war's prolongation was not driven by national interest or military necessity—it was fuelled by the regime's desire to preserve itself through manufactured external threats and ideological fervour. The lesson from this dark chapter in modern

---

[41] Rezai: Iranian forces should not have entered Iraq after liberation of Khorramshahr," Radio Farda, 25 September 2016. Available at https://www.radiofarda.com/a/f8-rezaee-war/28011425.html

Iranian history is clear: when governance is dictated by dogma rather than diplomacy, and ideology outweighs the welfare of a nation, war becomes not a last resort, but a political strategy. It is a lesson paid for dearly by a generation of Iranians.

Accepting the ceasefire was a political and ideological defeat for Khomeini and his regime. This cup of poison led to Khomeini's death 10 and a half months later. In an apparent attempt to reassert internal control and eliminate opposition, Khomeini ordered the mass execution of an estimated 30,000 political prisoners, primarily affiliated with the PMOI/MEK. However, the regime was once again rescued by regional developments, this time, by Saddam Hussein's invasion of Kuwait in August 1990. This act of aggression upended regional dynamics. Western powers, now focused on confronting Iraq, shifted their posture and opened channels of engagement with Tehran. The subsequent weakening of Iraq after the 1991 Gulf War enabled Tehran to extend its influence across the region, particularly in Iraq.

The U.S. invasion and occupation of Iraq in 2003 proved to be an unintended strategic windfall for the Iranian regime. It dismantled Iraq's state institutions and created a power vacuum that the Iranian regime quickly exploited, extending its ideological, political, and military reach to the borders of Israel, Lebanon, Saudi Arabia, and Jordan. What the regime failed to achieve in the 1980s with a million deaths, it achieved at the lowest price. In retrospect, the survival and consolidation of the Iranian regime over the past three and a half decades can be traced to two pivotal geopolitical developments: Iraq's 1990 invasion of Kuwait and the 2003 U.S. occupation of Iraq.

5

"Meet the new boss, same as the old boss."
— *Pete Townshend, The Who, "Won't Get Fooled Again"*

WHY THE IRGC MUST BE BLACKLISTED AND DISMANTLED

The IRGC's Iron Grip: Enforcing Repression and Terror

Founded in 1979 following the Iranian Revolution, the Islamic Revolutionary Guard Corps (IRGC) is notorious as a fearsome 'Gestapo-like' organization, renowned for brutally suppressing and murdering Iranian protesters and fomenting conflicts throughout the Middle East through its proxy allies. The IRGC is answerable directly to the Supreme Leader – Ayatollah Ali Khamenei, granting it substantial influence. Its roles include internal security, protecting the Iranian regime, controlling strategic military systems, and conducting asymmetric and unconventional warfare. The IRGC is focused on defending the regime from internal and external threats. This includes suppressing uprisings, controlling dissent, monitoring opposition groups, and enforcing ideological loyalty among the population. The IRGC is deeply embedded in Iran's political and security apparatus, often operating as the regime's enforcer.

Externally, the IRGC — especially through its elite Quds Force — plays a key role in projecting the Iranian regime's power across the region. It supports militant groups such as Hezbollah in Lebanon, Hamas in Gaza, the Shi'ite militias in Iraq, the former Assad regime in Syria, and the Houthi rebels in Yemen.

Of course, the IRGC and its Quds Force have not limited themselves to Shi'ite militias. They have also supported Sunni terrorist groups and recruited them for strategic purposes. Some of the leaders of al-Qaeda have been in Iran for many years and reportedly remain there today.[42]

On July 31, 2022, Ayman al-Zawahiri was killed by a U.S. drone strike in Kabul, Afghanistan, though neither Al Qaeda nor the Taliban formally acknowledged his death. Al Qaeda also failed to announce Zawahiri's successor, though United Nations sanctions monitors and others assessed that the de facto leader of the group is Sayf al-Adl. Al-Adl reportedly resides in Iran; Iran's government has allowed some Al Qaeda figures to operate in its territory despite historical animosity between Sunni

---

[42] "Al Qaeda: Background, Current Status, and U.S. Policy," Congressional Research Service, 5 June 2024. Available at: https://www.congress.gov/crs-product/IF11854

Al Qaeda and Iran's Shi'ite Islamic Republic. Al Qaeda leaders may view Iran as relatively safe from U.S. counterterrorism pressure, while Iranian leaders may view Al Qaeda's presence as leverage against the United States, as well as an opportunity to support another U.S. adversary.

This encroachment continues even as far away as Nigeria. With money and other incentives, the IRGC recruits a group of Shi'ites and organizes the Nigerian Hezbollah with them. These efforts are part of the regime's strategy in asymmetric warfare. A regime that lacks the capacity to confront its enemies in terms of classical military power (fighters, tanks, and other equipment) has sought to extort money through hostage-taking and to exert influence and domination over the countries of the region from day one, together with the creation of a network of proxies that can attack Iran's enemies without triggering a conventional war. Through these domestic and foreign operations, the IRGC has become one of the most powerful and influential institutions in the country and indeed in the Middle East.

The IRGC is estimated to have more than 190,000 personnel, including a ground force, a naval branch, an aerospace division (which includes Iran's ballistic missile program), and cyber warfare and intelligence units.[43] In addition to its regular forces, the IRGC oversees the Basij militia, a broad militia used to control civil unrest, impose loyalty, and mobilize public support for the regime.[44]

In addition to its military and security roles, the IRGC commands significant economic power, with control over large sectors of Iran's economy through foundations like Khatam al-Anbiya, which controls an estimated 40% of Iran's construction and energy sectors,[45] generating $10–15 billion annually in illicit revenue, according to a 2020 report. Senior corrupt IRGC commanders are known to have plundered billions, while millions of Iranians live below the poverty line, according to the World Bank.[46]

These criminals enjoy a luxurious lifestyle with foreign villas in Turkey, Dubai, and in Western countries such as Canada. Their children often attend

---

[43] Pemberton Jake, "Explainer: Iran's IRGC – A Force to Reckon With." i24NEWS, 22 April 2022. Available at:
https://www.i24news.tv/en/news/middle-east/iran-eastern-states/1650373743-explainer-iran-s-irgc

[44] National Council of Resistance of Iran U.S. Representative Office. *The Rise of Iran's Revolutionary Guards' Financial Empire: How the Supreme Leader and the IRGC Rob the People to Fund International Terror*. NCRI-US, 2017.

[45] Behnam Ben Taleblu, "The IRGC's Role in the Black Economy," NSI, Inc. (prepared for U.S. Central Command, citing FDD research), December 2020.

[46] Iran Poverty Diagnostic, Poverty and Shared Prosperity, the World Bank, Report No. 185679, November 2023.
https://documents1.worldbank.org/curated/en/099110623175541902/pdf/P1777150fa1dcd02108b55086af5f3268f5.pdf

Western schools and universities. The number of children of regime officials now in Western countries is so high that some of the regime's members have raised their voices in concern. On 31 October 2022, the regime's official news agency IRNA quoted Hajar Chinarani, a member of the regime's parliament, as saying that the number of the regime's children abroad was 5,400 and Morteza Mirian, the head of the IRGC's Ground Operations Department, at 4,000.[47]

The IRGC aerospace force controls Iran's missile forces and conducts conventional and strategic missile launches and drone operations. IRGC commanders manage missile brigades, drone units, and radar and satellite operations, supplying drones and drone technology and training to Russia for the war in Ukraine and to the Houthi rebels in Yemen, for use against commercial shipping, disrupting world trade. The EU, UK and U.S. admit that they have credible intelligence that Iran has supplied Russia with new surface-to-surface 4th generation Khorramshahr ballistic missiles called Kheibar, with a range of 2,000 km, distributed by the IRGC's aerospace force.

The IRGC has also become increasingly active in cyber warfare, targeting infrastructure, financial institutions, media, and dissident networks abroad. Its elite cyber units have targeted critical

---

[47] Official News Agency, IRNA, 31 October 2022.

infrastructure, including U.S. and European systems, Israeli firms, and healthcare networks, aiming to disrupt and intimidate, as reported by cybersecurity agencies.[48]

These state-sanctioned operations are not simply about information theft or disruption—they are designed to undermine trust in democratic institutions and intimidate civil society. The same tactics are deployed against Iranian dissidents in exile, with coordinated campaigns of digital harassment, hacking, and psychological intimidation. These cyber operations extend the IRGC's reach far beyond the Middle East, making it a global threat to digital security and human rights.

In 2025, the IRGC's malign activities intensified. In January, IRGC cyber units breached Australia's national power grid, causing widespread outages in Sydney to signal Iran's global reach, as reported by the Australian Cyber Security Centre (ACSC Alert, 2025). Concurrently, the Quds Force orchestrated a Houthi drone attack on a Saudi oil facility in February 2022, disrupting 5% of global oil supply, per Saudi Aramco's emergency statement. These incidents underscored

---

[48] Cybersecurity and Infrastructure Security Agency. "AA24-241A: Iran-Based Cyber Actors Enabling Ransomware Attacks on U.S. Organizations." August 20, 2024.
https://www.cisa.gov/news-events/cybersecurity-advisories/aa24-241a

the IRGC's unrelenting threat to international security and economic stability.

Simultaneously, the IRGC is deepening its strategic engagement in Latin America, where it collaborates with autocratic regimes such as Venezuela. Through its proxy Hezbollah, which maintains a logistical and financial network in South America's Tri-Border Area, the IRGC is involved in arms trafficking, money laundering, and intelligence gathering. These activities are not only funding terrorism but also giving the regime in Tehran a foothold in the Western Hemisphere - a dangerous development that has largely flown under the radar of Western policy. If left unchecked, the IRGC's expanding influence in Latin America could become a long-term strategic challenge, enabling Iran to threaten U.S. and European interests from much closer to home.

With the help of these networks, the Revolutionary Guards were able to carry out the great crime of the Argentine Israelite Mutual Association (AMIA) and the massacre of innocent people in Buenos Aires, Argentina, in 1994. The same criminal operation for which the Argentine prosecutor recently requested an arrest warrant for Khamenei.

The lead prosecutor in the case of the 1994 bombing of the AMIA Jewish community centre in Buenos Aires has petitioned Argentina's federal court to issue national and international arrest warrants for Iran's so-called "supreme leader," Ayatollah Ali Khamenei, over his alleged involvement in the deadly terrorist attack.[49]

In 2024, Venezuelan authorities uncovered an IRGC-backed Hezbollah arms smuggling ring in Caracas, trafficking weapons to Colombian militias, as reported by the U.S. Southern Command.

The Basij is widely hated by the Iranian population, as it is comprised largely of ill-educated thugs who specialize in vicious attacks on protesters and demonstrators, targeting women in particular. In February 2025, Basij forces violently dispersed a student protest in Isfahan, killing 8 and arresting 300, as documented by Amnesty International (Amnesty International, 2025).

With an estimated 1 million volunteers organized into 50,000 local cells, the Basij brutally suppressed a 2024 women's protest in Tehran, killing 12 and injuring 200, as reported by Iran Human Rights (IHR, 2024).

---

[49] Vilches Arguello, Ailin. "Argentina Prosecutor Seeks Arrest Warrants for Iran's Supreme Leader Over 1994 AMIA Bombing." The Algemeiner, 9 April 2025. Available at: https://www.algemeiner.com/2025/04/09/argentina-prosecutor-seeks-arrest-warrants-irans-supreme-leader-1994-amia-bombing/

The IRGC Navy conducts asymmetric naval warfare, including the use of small fast boats and submarines. Specialized in guerrilla naval tactics, mine warfare, and the use of speedboats, IRGC personnel have threatened U.S. military vessels, attached limpet mines to commercial oil-tankers, seized commercial vessels in pirate-style attacks and generally disrupted traffic in the Persian Gulf and the Strait of Hormuz. The Quds force was commanded by General Qassem Soleimani, killed by an American drone attack in January 2020, as he emerged in a convoy from Baghdad Airport.

In April 2025, a Hezbollah cell, directed by the Quds Force, attempted to bomb a Jewish cultural centre in Paris, foiled by French intelligence, highlighting the IRGC's persistent European terror campaign, per France's General Directorate for Internal Security (DGSI) - (DGSI Alert, 2025).

Illicit Empire and Global Menace: The Case for Action

The IRGC has also played a central role in the international drugs trade, laundering dirty money for gangsters and cartel Godfathers, helping the mullahs to overcome the impact of western sanctions, and providing the regime with the means to finance and supply its terrorist proxies. There is growing evidence that the Iranian regime works closely with the Taliban boosting the Afghan drug trade. Afghanistan produces over 80% of the world's opium, with significant quantities transiting through Iran, according to UN reports.[50]

Before Assad's fall, the IRGC had set up a vast drug production organization (including Captagon pills) in Syria, from which it exported to Arab countries, the Persian Gulf states, and even Europe.[51]

The U.S. Treasury Department has in the past sanctioned specific IRGC commanders for suspected involvement in drug trafficking. Through these sinister links, the theocratic regime has been able to exploit international organized crime networks, turning them into a political force that runs terrorist activities around the world, while circumventing transnational scrutiny and economic sanctions. The billions of dollars flowing into Iran from these drug cartels, has provided the Iranian regime with the means to finance its proxies like Hezbollah, Hamas, the Houthis and the Iraqi militias, bolstering their destabilizing agendas, promoting their ideological objectives and sowing chaos on a global scale.

---

[50] NDTV, "Afghanistan Account For 80% Of Global Illicit Opium Production In 2022: UN Report," 27 June 2023. Available at: https://www.ndtv.com/world-news/afghanistan-account-for-80-of-global-illicit-opium-production-in-2022-un-report-4155346

[51] Rogin, Josh. "Assad's Drug Empire Is Funding Iranian-Backed Militias and Fueling Hamas." *The Washington Post*, November 13, 2023. Available at:
https://hill.house.gov/news/documentsingle.aspx?DocumentID=9218

Tehran is happy to provide money laundering facilities for the drug barons in exchange for criminal services overseas, including assassinations, bombings, and kidnappings. According to the U.S. Treasury Department: "The MOIS and Iran's Islamic Revolutionary Guard Corps (IRGC) have long targeted perceived regime opponents in acts of transnational repression outside of Iran, a practice that the regime has accelerated in recent years.

A wide range of dissidents, journalists, activists, and former Iranian officials have been targeted for assassination, kidnapping, and hacking operations across numerous countries in the Middle East, Europe, and North America. The regime increasingly relies on organized criminal groups in furtherance of these plots in an attempt to obscure links to the Government of Iran and maintain plausible deniability.

Last year, the U.S. Drug Enforcement Agency offered a $5 million reward for information leading to the capture of Christy Kinahan Snr and each of his two sons, Daniel and Christy Jnr. They are the Irish leaders of one of the world's biggest drug cartels, with a base in Kish Island, a tiny Iranian enclave 12 miles off the mainland coast, known as the 'Pearl of the Persian Gulf'.

The Kinahan's and other drug barons use the island to launder their billions in dirty drugs money and in return, carry out assassinations on behalf of the Ministry of Intelligence and Security (MOIS) and the IRGC. Kish Island is a Free Trade Zone, known as Iran's Costa Del Sol and while women have to wear headscarves and traditional costumes, the paradise island has a more European feel, with alcohol served in hotels and restaurants and a huge coral beach for snorkelling. It is also beyond the reach of international drug enforcement agencies.

The repeated failure of Western governments to confront the Iranian regime with meaningful consequences has emboldened the clerical establishment in Tehran, allowing it to expand its regional aggression and internal repression unchecked. For over four decades, Western policy—particularly that of the European Union—has been defined by appeasement: a cycle of concessions, economic incentives, and misguided hopes of moderation that have only reinforced the regime's belief that it can act with impunity. At the heart of this machinery of terror stands the Islamic Revolutionary Guard Corps (IRGC) and the Ministry of Intelligence (MOIS), the regime's principal tools for enforcing its will both at home and abroad.

The IRGC, which has more facilities and mercenary groups, has organised terrorism across the Middle East, interfered in European affairs, and helped prop up dictatorships and proxy militias in Syria, Lebanon, Iraq, Gaza, and Yemen. Within Iran, it has crushed uprisings, detained and tortured thousands, and acted as the iron fist of Supreme Leader Ali Khamenei in silencing any demand for democracy.

Critics argue that designating the IRGC as a terrorist organization could escalate tensions and disrupt nuclear negotiations, but such concerns prioritize short-term diplomacy over the long-term threat of an unchecked IRGC fuelling global instability. The European Union and the United Kingdom must join the United States and Canada in officially designating the IRGC as a terrorist organisation. Continued refusal to do so sends a dangerous message of weakness and indifference—not only to the regime in Tehran, but to the Iranian people risking their lives for freedom. Arguing that such a move would hinder diplomatic dialogue is not only morally bankrupt, but also strategically naïve.

Why maintain dialogue with a regime that openly calls for the destruction of Western values and engages in hostage-taking and state-sponsored terrorism? Instead, the West must engage with the democratic opposition. Blacklisting and dismantling the IRGC is not merely a necessary step to halt its external terror activities—it is also an essential act of solidarity with a nation striving to reclaim its future.

6

"The evil that men do lives after them."
— *William Shakespeare, Julius Caesar*

THE RISE AND FALL OF QASSEM SOLEIMANI

Architect of Terror: Soleimani's Brutal Ascendancy

Maj. Gen. Qassem Soleimani was one of the top military commanders and one of the most powerful figures in the Iranian regime. He was described as the regime's No. 2 after Khamenei. Born on March 13, 1957, Soleimani was a major general in the Islamic Revolutionary Guard Corps (IRGC) and commander of the Quds Force - a division primarily responsible for military and covert cross-border operations, from 1998 until his death on 3 January 2020.

The initial cells of the Quds Force were formed during the Iran-Iraq War. At that time, the IRGC's overseas forces were operating deep inside Iraqi territory under the name of Camp Ramadan. These post-war overseas units took on the name of the Quds Force after the war in the early 1990s. For the first time, the

Mojahedin Organization announced an entity called the Quds Force.[52]

The first commander of the IRGC's Quds Force was Brigadier General Vahidi. But he was replaced in 1997 by IRGC Brig. Gen. Qassem Soleimani, who turned the force into a hegemonic force in the region for 22 years until he was killed by the United States in January 2020.

He was in the IRGC from the beginning of the formation of the clerical regime. He led a military group during the Iran-Iraq war and quickly rose through the ranks and eventually became the commander of the 41st Division of Tharallah, when he was about 25 years old. He took part in almost all of the major battles of the war, mostly stationed on the Southern Front.

---

[52] Mohaddessin, Mohammad. *Islamic Fundamentalism: The New Global Threat*. Seven Locks Press, 2001. Available at: https://www.amazon.com/Islamic-Fundamentalism-New-Global-Threat/dp/092976532X

Caption: Supreme Leader Khamenei is pictured alongside General Qassem Soleimani and Hezbollah leader Hassan Nasrallah in what appears to be a symbolic gathering. (Photo: Khamenei.ir)

Soleimani's strategic acumen in command of the Quds Force allowed him to effectively expand Iran's influence throughout the Middle East. He was very successful in asymmetric warfare, intelligence operations and the building of proxy networks. He played a key role in supporting and organizing proxy militias in Lebanon (Hezbollah), Iraq (various Shia militias), Syria (supporting the Assad regime), Gaza (Hamas), and Yemen (the Houthis). By empowering these factions, he increased Iran's geopolitical reach. At the same time, despite the sectarian divide, he also leveraged tactical relationships with Sunni extremist groups such as al-Qaeda and ISIS.

It was the Iranian mullahs' support for the deeply corrupt then Prime Minister Nouri al-Maliki in Iraq[53] and for Bashar al-Assad in Syria,[54] two crooked and murderous dictators whose sectarian policies repressed their own people and particularly the Sunni communities in those two countries, that created fertile ground for the rise of Daesh (ISIS). Because the Sunnis were humiliated and brutally contained, they were driven into the arms of the Islamic extremists. In part due to Tehran's policies and sectarian support for authoritarian leaders,[55] conditions allowed ISIS to flourish, thus becoming a threat to the Middle East and to the whole world.

The Iranian regime exploited the war on Daesh as an opportunity to consolidate its policy of aggressive sectarian expansionism in the Middle East.[56] Claiming

---

[53] "Iran's Militia Allies in Iraq", Wilson Center, 2 February 2024. Available at: https://www.wilsoncenter.org/article/profiles-irans-militia-allies-iraq

[54] Karim Sadjadpour, "Iran's Unwavering Support to Assad's Syria", 27 August 2013, Carnegie Endowment for International Peace. Available at:
https://carnegieendowment.org/posts/2013/09/irans-unwavering-support-to-assads-syria?lang=en

[55] Callum Paton, "Iran trains thousands of mercenaries each year to fight in Syria and Iraq wars claims PMOI", International Business Times, 14 February 2017. Available at:
https://www.ibtimes.co.uk/iran-trains-thousands-mercenaries-each-year-fight-syria-iraq-wars-claims-pmoi-1606591

[56] According to an analysis by the Center for Strategic & International Studies: "In addition, Iraqi nationalism and anti-Iranian sentiments among Iraqis continues to linger from the Iran-Iraq War. Some public opinion polls indicate that many Iraqis are highly critical of Iran's role in the country.67 In Sunni

to help the West to fight terrorists, Iran's Supreme Leader Ayatollah Ali Khamenei ordered Qassem Soleimani and his Quds Force cohorts to lead a genocidal onslaught on the Sunni communities of Iraq. Thousands of Sunnis were murdered, and the ancient Iraqi cities of Ramadi, Fallujah and Mosul were left as smoking ruins, with mainly women and children among the few survivors.[57]

Western powers, often misreading the sectarian dimensions of the region, inadvertently supported the regime's brutal campaigns by providing air cover and conducting bombing raids on these ancient Iraqi cities, which were reduced to rubble.

By concentrating its efforts on obtaining a predominant position in Iraq, Lebanon, and Syria, the Iranian regime persistently sought to secure pathways traversing Iran's western borders through the Euphrates and Tigris valleys and the vast expanses of

---

areas like Al-Anbar Province, locals bitterly complain about the proliferation of Shia militias, feel alienated from a government in Baghdad they believe is too closely aligned with Shia, and protest the slow pace of reconstruction following the collapse of the Islamic State's so-called caliphate. As one Iraqi intelligence official acknowledged, "This is not just revenge on ISIS. This is revenge on Sunnis."" Seth G. Jones, "War by Proxy: Iran's Growing Footprint in the Middle East," CSIS, 11 March 2019. Available at: https://www.csis.org/analysis/war-proxy-irans-growing-footprint-middle-east

[57] Amnesty International, "Iraq: Absolute Impunity: Militia Rule in Iraq", 14 October 2014. Available at: https://www.amnesty.org/en/documents/MDE14/015/2014/en/

desert in Iraq and Syria. This provided a logistical link to Hezbollah in Lebanon and finally ending at the edge of the Golan Heights. These corridors were designed to serve as conduits through which military supplies and military personnel could be sent to the battlefronts where Iranian proxies were actively engaged. To this end, dozens of Quds Force affiliated military and political bases were formed west of Mosul, under the guise of the Iraqi Popular Mobilization Forces (PMF), a state-sanctioned umbrella organisation comprising primarily Shi'ite militias overseen by Soleimani.[58]

Nationwide protests also raged across Iraq where young Iraqis demanded an end to Iranian interference in their country and the expulsion of Soleimani and his allies. In February 2018, at the height of the protests, Soleimani said in a speech in Kerman that the Iranian regime "has rubbed the enemy's nose in the dirt during the 2009 sedition and the recent unrest."[59] In Iraq, he deployed masked gunmen to

---

[58] Ranj Alaaldin, "The Popular Mobilization Force is turning Iraq into an Iranian client state" Brookings Institute, 2 February 2024. Available at: https://www.brookings.edu/articles/the-popular-mobilization-force-is-turning-iraq-into-an-iranian-client-state/

[59] State-run Tasnim news agency (in Farsi), 11 February 2018. Available at:
https://www.tasnimnews.com/fa/news/1396/11/22/1653838/کر-مان-سرلشکر-سلیمانی-ملت-ایران-در-فتنه-۸۸-و-اغتشاشات-اخیر-بینی-دشمن-را-به-خاک-مالید-باید-کف-پای-این-ملت-را-بوسید

murder hundreds of peaceful demonstrators as well.[60] It is no surprise that tens of thousands of young Iraqis took to the streets to celebrate the elimination of Soleimani and Abu Mahdi al-Muhandis.[61]

Soleimani was personally involved in coordinating Iran's regional strategy and was known for his ability to forge strong personal relationships with local leaders and commanders, fostering loyalty and facilitating effective collaboration. Regarded as a hero by many of the regime's supporters within Iran, his actions and persona were portrayed as defending Iran's interests and security against foreign adversaries. Although Soleimani orchestrated widespread atrocities and regional destabilisation, the Iranian regime and its proxies propagated a narrative portraying him as a defender against foreign threats and ISIS terrorists -an image that belies the

---

[60] According to Amnesty International, the Iran-backed "Popular Mobilization Units (PMU), a large network of militias legally considered part of the Iraqi Armed Forces, used lethal force against protesters and pursued a sinister campaign of extrajudicial killings and enforced disappearances." See "Iraq: Four years after Tishreen protests, no justice for state and militia violence", Amnesty International, 27 September 2023. Available at: https://www.amnesty.org/en/latest/news/2023/09/iraq-four-years-after-tishreen-protests-no-justice-for-state-and-militia-violence/

[61] "Fear and joy on the streets of Baghdad after Soleimani killing", France24, 3 January 2020. Available at: https://www.france24.com/en/20200103-fear-and-joy-streets-baghdad-after-soleimani-killing-iraq-iran-usa-quds-revolutionary-guards

devastating human cost of his actions and highlights the regime's use of propaganda to mask its crimes.

For Khamenei, Soleimani was not just a military commander, but also a driver of his foreign policy, especially in the region. Mohammad Javad Zarif, the regime's foreign minister between 2013 and 2021, explained that he met with Soleimani on a weekly basis and took many lines from him and provided him with the facilities of the Foreign Ministry. In one instance, in August 2013, when Bashar al-Assad brutally targeted the Damascus suburb with chemical bombs, killing thousands of innocent civilians, President Obama announced that he would avenge this great crime. In the last days of August (most likely August 27 or 28), Soleimani rushed to Baghdad late at night and went directly to Prime Minister Nouri al-Maliki, with an offer to Washington.

Maliki's national security adviser, Falih Al-Fayyadh, immediately took the offer to Washington. The deal stated that the Iranian regime would agree to talks about its nuclear programme, and Syria's Bashar al-Assad would agree to dismantle his chemical weapons, in return for an understanding that the mullahs' regime would have the freedom to kill the residents of Camp Ashraf.

On August 31, while U.S. allies such as France were preparing to participate in a U.S. coordinated night operation against Bashar al-Assad, the Americans suddenly announced that the operation was cancelled. Obama's August 31 speech and his reneging on all his promises surprised everyone. In the early morning of September 1, 2013, Qassem Soleimani's forces attacked Ashraf, the headquarters of the principal opposition MEK, and killed 52 men and women, taking 7 people, including 6 women, who have never been heard from again, as hostages. The following month, the 5+1 Joint Comprehensive Plan of Action (JCPOA) nuclear negotiations began in Geneva! A dirty deal that added years to the life of the Syrian dictator and sacrificed the PMOI.

Fallen Tyrant: Soleimani's Demise and Demand for Justice

Tensions between the U.S. and Iran escalated sharply following President Trump's unilateral withdrawal from the Iran Nuclear Deal in 2018 and the subsequent reimposition of 'maximum pressure' sanctions. Soleimani was also believed to be orchestrating attacks against U.S. and allied interests in the region. On 3 January 2020, Soleimani was killed by a targeted U.S. drone strike near Baghdad International Airport in Iraq.[62] The strike also

---

[62] Zachary Cohen, Hamdi Alkhshali, Kareem Khadder and Angela Dewan, "US drone strike ordered by Trump kills top Iranian commander in Baghdad", CNN, 4 January 2020. Available at:
https://www.cnn.com/2020/01/02/middleeast/baghdad-airport-rockets/index.html

eliminated Abu Mahdi al-Muhandis, deputy commander of the Iranian-aligned Popular Mobilization Forces (PMF) in Iraq.

The elimination of Soleimani delivered a severe blow to the Iranian regime.[63] He was responsible for thousands of deaths among Iraqi, Syrian and Lebanese civilians as well as among U.S. military personnel. Soleimani was answerable only to Ayatollah Khamenei and as such, was the second most powerful figure in the Islamic Republic. As Qassem Soleimani and Abu Mahdi al-Muhandis discovered to their ultimate cost, there can be no impunity for those guilty of such chilling atrocities.

As the architect of Iran's regional proxy wars and the ruthless enforcer of internal oppression, Soleimani embodied the theocratic regime's vision of power through fear and violence. His actions left a trail of devastation across the Middle East, from the shattered cities of Iraq and Syria to the blood-soaked streets of Iranian towns and villages. His killing in January 2020 did not merely eliminate a military commander—it removed a central pillar of the regime's apparatus of terror, both at home and abroad.

---

[63] Ray Takeyh, "Soleimani's Death: A Crippling Blow to the Iranian Regime", Council on Foreign Relations, 3 January 2020. Available at: https://www.cfr.org/in-brief/soleimanis-death-crippling-blow-iranian-regime

Soleimani's fall was a turning point, exposing the vulnerability of a regime long shrouded in the myth of untouchable power.

But justice for Soleimani's victims cannot end with his death. The crimes committed under his command—against peaceful protesters, regional populations, and political prisoners—require formal international reckoning. The chapter of Soleimani's legacy should close not only with his elimination but with a renewed global commitment to confront and hold accountable the full machinery of repression he helped to build.

7

"You can chain a man's body, but you cannot chain his mind."
- *Thomas Sankara*

HOW IRAN MANAGED TO CONTROL THE IRAQI MILITIAS

Puppet Masters: Iran's Grip on Iraqi Militias

There are many factors that bind the people of Iran and Iraq, especially in southern and central Iraq. The vast majority of the people of southern Iraq are Shi'ites, many of whom are related to the Arabs of southern Iran. They are further bound by shared borders and mutual economic interests. The shrines of 6 Shi'ite Imams are in Iraq. Iranian pilgrims frequently travel to these religious sites. At the same time, the governments of these two countries have had many contradictions with each other throughout history. The reason for some of the wars between Iran and the Ottomans in the 17th, 18th, and 19th centuries was partly due to Iran's attention to these Shi'ite centres. Iraq was part of this domain before the collapse of the Ottoman Empire and the independence of Iraq. After Iraq's independence, there have been many conflicts and disputes between the two countries.

Due to religious reasons, a large population of Iranians has always lived in Iraq. Iranian governments, including the Shah's regime, leveraged the Iranian diaspora in Iraq to extend its influence. With the rise of the Ba'ath Party in Iraq, especially after 1968, these contradictions increased. In order to prevent Iran's influence, Iraq expelled a large number of Iranians living in Iraq from the country. It is said that the number of these Iranians amounted to hundreds of thousands. In Iran, these people were called Mu'awidin (returnees). These people, who had lost decades of their lives in Iraq and sometimes hundreds of years, had a double enmity with the Iraqi government.

As we have seen in the previous chapters, after gaining power in Iran, Khomeini tried to expand his power to Iraq, which derived from religious authority and the momentum of a popular revolution. At first, this attention was in the form of a call to the people of Iraq to disobey the Iraqi army, and to rise up and carry out terrorist acts. This effort, however, failed to gain traction. With the outbreak of the Iran-Iraq war, Khomeini tried to create an organized force of Iraqis against the Iraqi government.

The first important step in this regard was the formation of a group called the 9th Badr Corps in 1982. The group was rapidly integrated into the Iranian regime military apparatus. Khomeini appointed a powerful mullah named Mahmoud Hashemi Shahroudi to head the 9th Badr Corps. Notably, two decades later, the same Shahroudi was appointed as head of the Iranian regime's judiciary. In 1982, Khomeini appointed then-president Ali Khamenei as an observer of the 9th Badr Corps.[64]

The 9th Badr Corps gradually expanded and participated as part of the Revolutionary Guards in the war against Iraq and in the suppression of Iranian opponents. With the first Gulf War and the disruption of the regional balance of power between Iran and Iraq, the Iranian regime sought to expand Iraqi Shi'ite militias on the one hand, and on the other hand, given the situation in Iraqi Kurdistan, which was out of the practical control of the central government in Baghdad, sought to infiltrate the region and establish networks of loyal paramilitaries.

But after the U.S. invasion of Iraq in 2003 and the collapse of Iraq's military and administrative system, Tehran rapidly accelerated the expansion of its Shi'ite militia networks. The United States, which wanted to overthrow the Iraqi government in an erroneous

---

[64] State-run Kayhan newspaper, 17 November 17, 1982, Jomhuri Eslami newspaper, 18 November 1982.

policy, negotiated with the Iranian regime in order to get the mullahs help in the war. Representatives of the Iranian regime, the U.S. government, and the British ambassador in Geneva focused on this issue. The Iranian regime pledged to allow British and American warplanes to pass over western Iran, and also pledged not to interfere in Iraq after the overthrow of the Iraqi government. Britain and the United States agreed to target the bases of the Mujahedin-e Khalq (PMOI/MEK).[65] The United States and the United Kingdom fulfilled their commitment to the fullest, but the Iranian regime continued to interfere to the maximum in Iraq, especially with the help of these militias.

In 2005, the PMOI revealed a list of 32,000 Iraqi mercenaries employed by the Iranian regime inside Iraq. The list included the names of the mercenaries, their place of work, their salaries, their account numbers, and many other details. These were the backbone of the Iraqi militias. Although this list was also in the possession of the United States, U.S. officials showed no interest in neutralizing them, misguidedly calculating that Shi'ite militias could be used to resist Sunni militias.

---

[65] Cummings, Jeanne. "U.S. Bombs Iranian Fighters on Iraqi Side of the Border." The Wall Street Journal, 17 April 2003. Available at:
https://www.wsj.com/articles/SB105053141922836600

Some militias were formed with direct Iranian backing. For example, the Badr Organisation was originally established by Iran's IRGC during the Iran-Iraq war.[66] Iran supplied arms, training, and tactical support to these militias. The IRGC's Quds Force has been instrumental in providing this military assistance and has funnelled an estimated $1 billion annually to Iraqi militias, according to U.S. intelligence reports. Iran has also funnelled financial resources to these groups, which helps ensure their loyalty and operational capability.

Iran has backed Shi'ite political parties in Iraq, providing them with both military equipment and financial support and guidance. This support helps these parties gain power in the Iraqi government, indirectly ensuring Iranian political influence. By establishing strong links with key politicians, Iran ensured that its interests were represented within the Iraqi political system. This became particularly evident during the tenure of Prime Minister Nouri al-Maliki, who effectively became an Iranian puppet. Exerting control over Shi'ite militias in Iraq further embedded the Iranian regime, serving as a direct counterweight to U.S. presence and influence both within Iraq and across the broader region. Through these militias -organised under the umbrella of the

---

[66] "Profile: Badr Organization", The Washington Institute for Near East Policy, 2 September 2021. Available at: https://www.washingtoninstitute.org/policy-analysis/profile-badr-organization

Popular Mobilization Forces (PMF) -Iran was able to project power in Iraq without direct military confrontation.[67]

Formally established in 2014 following a call to mobilization by Grand Ayatollah Ali al-Sistani to combat the rise of Daesh (ISIS), the Popular Mobilization Forces soon evolved beyond their initial defensive mandate. While they incorporated a broad array of militias - some with purely Iraqi nationalist motivations - Tehran actively ensured that the most powerful factions remained under its influence. Groups such as Kata'ib Hezbollah, Asa'ib Ahl al-Haq, and the Badr Organisation received direct guidance, training, and financial support from Iran's IRGC-Quds Force, effectively embedding Tehran's agenda within the PMF's command structure.

Almost turning Iraq into an Iranian province, the Iranian regime established significant economic links with Iraq, including $10 billion in annual trade and infrastructure projects, fostering influence that bolsters allied militias such as the PMF.[68]

---

[67] Ranj Alaaldin, "The Popular Mobilization Force is turning Iraq into an Iranian client state" Brookings Institute, 2 February 2024. Available at: https://www.brookings.edu/articles/the-popular-mobilization-force-is-turning-iraq-into-an-iranian-client-state/
[68] Islamic Republic News Agency, IRNA, "Iran-Iraq annual bilateral trade exceeds $10 billion, 3 September 2024. Available at:
https://en.irna.ir/news/85586071/Iran-Iraq-annual-bilateral-trade-exceeds-10-billion

In an effort to foster goodwill, Iran often engaged in development aid and social services projects in Shi'ite majority areas, underpinning its influence. The mullahs' regime established cultural centres, and funded educational institutions, as well as promoting pilgrimages to religious sites in Iran, to serve as soft power tools to enhance Iran's overall influence. In a coordinated public relations campaign, Iranian media disseminates pro-Iranian narratives that resonate with Iraq's Shi'ite communities.

Iran's dominance over the Popular Mobilization Forces in Iraq is not due to a single factor. Through a complex interplay of religious ties, political maneuvering, military assistance, and financial backing, Gen. Qassem Soleimani was instrumental in shaping Shi'ite militias into a useful proxy tool, enabling Iran to maintain a significant degree of control and influence over these groups and the broader sociopolitical landscape in Iraq. Sunni communities, marginalized by Iranian-backed governments, often see the PMF as a sectarian enforcer that fuels insurgency and instability.

However, the PMF's transformation into a sprawling quasi-state actor with parallel military, economic, and political capabilities has increasingly alarmed many Iraqis. Despite claims of allegiance to Baghdad, many Iran-aligned PMF factions operate independently of the central government, undermining national sovereignty. Their ability to control checkpoints, extract taxes, and even administer their own territories has fuelled accusations that Iraq has become a patchwork of militia-controlled fiefdoms beholden to Tehran rather than Baghdad.

However, recent events have revealed growing cracks in Iran's regional strategy. While Tehran invested heavily in exporting its revolutionary model and fostering a network of loyal militias, the 2023 Gaza war exposed the vulnerability of this approach. Iran's proxies, including Hezbollah and the Houthis, demonstrated symbolic support for the Palestinian cause but fell short of delivering the unified, decisive resistance Iran had long promised. This hesitancy reflected not only strategic caution but a recognition that the cost of direct confrontation had become unsustainable for both Iran and its allies.

But before that, and more importantly, not only have Iraq's Sunnis grown increasingly resentful of the Iranian regime's covert occupation, there is also rising hostility toward the Iranian regime among Iraqi Shi'ites, particularly among the youth, which narrows the operating space for IRGC-affiliated militias. While the trajectory of Iraq's current conflict remains uncertain and contingent on numerous factors, it is certain that the regime's influence in Iraq will be less than in the past.

The IRGC's traditional strategy of outsourcing conflicts through local militias has increasingly failed and has severely weakened Iran's position both regionally and domestically.

Iraq's Burden: Resisting Iran's Shadow Empire

Before his death, Qassem Soleimani developed a two-pronged approach to consolidate Iran's control over Iraq. Firstly, and of key importance, he was determined to prevent Baghdad from ever again becoming hostile to Tehran, as had occurred under Saddam Hussein, leading to the 1980-88 war. Soleimani's second key goal was to drive U.S. forces out of Iraq and out of the region at large.

The leading cleric in Iraq is the 94-year-old Iranian-born Grand Ayatollah Ali al-Sistani. He has advocated for Iraqi sovereignty and has rejected *velãyat-e faqih*, rallying nationalist sentiments against Iranian overreach. He does not think that clerics should be involved in politics. Al-Sistani's insistence on the separation of religious authority from political power has served as an important counterweight to Iranian influence in Iraq, advocating a vision of governance rooted in national identity rather than sectarian domination.

Iran and Iraq also enjoy strong trade ties. In 2021, Iraq was Iran's second-largest export market after China. Iraq also relies on Iran for natural gas and electricity imports, and the U.S. exempts it from sanctions applied to Iran's energy sector.

Following its eight-year occupation of Iraq, the U.S. sought to establish the formation of a strong government in Baghdad that could withstand threats to its sovereignty from Iran. The Americans were also keen to preserve access to Iraq's vast energy resources. In reality, both the U.S. and Iran continue to jostle for influence in Iraq, though Iraqi leaders often view Tehran as a more dependable partner than Washington. Other Arab nations have also shown an interest in improving relations with Iraq, in a bid to lessen Iran's influence. Saudi Arabia, a longtime rival of the Iranian regime, has made considerable efforts to strengthen its relationship with Baghdad.

But as long as these armed militias remain under the sway of the Islamic Republic, Iraq's prospects for peace, reform, and independence remain bleak. For the people of Iraq - who have time and again risen in protest against Iranian meddling- true liberation will only come when the influence of the *velâyat-e faqih* system is dismantled, and the sovereignty of Iraq is returned to its rightful owners: the Iraqi people.

8

"The blood of the martyrs is the seed of tyranny's end."
— *Adapted from Tertullian*

WHY DID IRAN SUPPORT BASHAR AL-ASSAD IN SYRIA?

Lifeline to a Tyrant: Iran's Stake in Assad's Syria

The Iranian regime supported Bashar al-Assad in Syria for several strategic and geopolitical reasons. First, Iran aimed to increase its influence in the Middle East. Supporting Assad was crucial for maintaining and expanding Iran's presence in Syria, which was seen as a critical ally in a region where Iran sought to counterbalance rivals like Saudi Arabia and extend its influence over the Arab world. Syria under Assad had long been a close ally of Iran, providing a corridor for Iranian authority into Lebanon, where Hezbollah, a key proxy backed by Iran, operated. Maintaining Assad's regime helped ensure that this alliance remained solid and that the logistical links between Iran and Hezbollah were preserved. The sudden and unexpected fall of the Assad regime changed everything for Iran.

Relations between the Iranian regime and the Assad family date back to the first weeks and months of the theocratic dictatorship in Iran. Khomeini, with a shrewd sense for political opportunity, took advantage of the enmity between the two branches of the Ba'ath Party in Iraq and Syria and forged a strategic alliance with Hafez al-Assad, father of Bashar al-Assad. Since the beginning of the Iran-Iraq war in 1980, Damascus sided with Tehran, and was the first state to supply Iran with Soviet-made Scud missiles.

In order to understand the relationship between Syria and the Iranian regime in the 1980s, the report of the Tasnim News Agency, which is affiliated with the terrorist Quds Force, on December 13, 2015, says in part:

"During the war, Syria was one of the few countries that supported Iran and provided extensive military and political support to our country. Syria provided our country with significant military, political and intelligence assistance. Missile experts went to Syria for training, and many of Iraq's maps and Iraqi military intelligence were provided to our country by Syria.

Syria's support for Iran in the imposed war had a special effect. Syria's most important contribution in the war was its political support for Iran, because Syria's positions at the Arab Conference prevented the formation of a united front of Arab countries against the Islamic Republic of Iran.

In supplying Iran with weapons during the imposed war and while heavy arms embargoes were imposed on our country, Syria during the era of Hafez al-Assad had a very special position. According to Iranian officials, Syria was one of the source countries for supplying weapons and equipment to Iran during the war. In this regard, Mohsen Rafiqdoust believes that Iran's first arms purchase from the Eastern Bloc was made during the time of the late Hafez al-Assad. A part of Damascus International Airport was allocated to the Islamic Republic of Iran.

Due to the heavy arms embargo imposed on the Islamic Republic, it was impossible to purchase missiles, and especially to acquire their knowledge. In such circumstances, Syria was the only country that gave Tehran the green light. This also led to the first sparks of indigenous missile knowledge in our country from Syria.

Since the Iranian team was stationed in the country's most important missile barracks on the direct orders of then-Syrian President Hafez al-Assad, the Iranian team took advantage of every opportunity for training so that the members went to ammunition dumps, missile depots, etc.

It was with these trainings that Iran's missile knowledge was sparked, and during the war, with Scud missiles purchased from Libya at that time, our country was able to target Baghdad and create a balance in the discussion of urban warfare between the two countries.

One of the most important measures taken by Syria under Hafez al-Assad to support the Islamic Republic of Iran and put pressure on Iraq was to cut off the Iraqi oil pipeline to the Mediterranean Sea. Due to its very limited land border with the Persian Gulf and the complete destruction of its navy, Iraq resorted to using land lines, including the pipeline that ran from Basra to the Mediterranean Sea. The pipeline, which supplied tankers with Iraqi oil (at a rate of 500,000 barrels per day), was of vital importance to Baghdad.

In order to defend Iran, Syria completely blocked the pipeline in 1982, causing Iraq's oil revenues to drop by 30 percent. This blow was so severe for the Ba'ath regime in Iraq that it immediately increased its efforts to overthrow the Syrian government and began arming the Muslim Brotherhood forces on Syrian soil.

During the Iran-Iraq war, another measure taken by the Syrian government in support of Iran was to provide information to identify the military bases of the Iraqi forces as well as the Russian weapons used by Iraq. This information, along with the missile training that was given to Iranian experts, was very important for our country and played a very important role in Iran's victories against Saddam's invasion."[69]

From a strategic point of view, Syria's importance to the regime was the connection to the Mediterranean Sea, active access to Lebanon, and its border with Israel. Following Iran's de facto control over Iraq, the regime took control of Syria and formed what King Abdullah of Jordan called the Shi'ite crescent - a crescent that is made up of Iran, Iraq, Syria, and Lebanon and has strategic consequences for the entire Middle East.

Therefore, Iran's Supreme Leader Ayatollah Ali Khamenei saw Syria as a vital ally and an extremely important link in his regional and international strategy. For decades, the Islamic Revolutionary Guard Corps (IRGC) provided significant military support, including militias, to prop up Assad's regime

---

[69] "Why Did Syria Provide Military Support to Iran During the Iran-Iraq War." Tasnim News Agency, December 13, 2015. Available at:
https://www.tasnimnews.com/fa/news/1394/09/22/941583/چرا-سوریه-در-زمان-دفاع-مقدس-به-ایران-کمک-نظامی-کرد

(Al Jazeera, 2024). The sudden collapse of the Assad dictatorship removed a fundamental pillar vital for the Islamic Republic's regional strategy and disrupted its regional posture. It eroded public confidence in Iran's regime, with protests in Tehran decrying wasted billions, while Iranian-backed militias questioned Tehran's reliability.

Hezbollah, the Shi'ite militant group and political party based in Lebanon, was a major ally of both Iran and the Assad regime.[70] The fall of Assad undermined Iran's capacity to support Hezbollah, which served Iranian interests by acting as a deterrent against Israel and Western influence in the region. While Iran prioritized Shi'ite militias, it also sought to co-opt Sunni tribes in Aleppo and Raqqa by offering economic inducements.

Despite its Shi'ite ideological core, Iran pragmatically extended its outreach to select Sunni groups in Syria, offering financial incentives and military support in an attempt to expand its influence and gain broader local legitimacy.

For the Iranian regime, Assad's Syria provided a vital geographic supply route for Hezbollah. Hezbollah's political and military capabilities improved

---

[70] See, for example: "Syrian town of Qusair falls to Hezbollah in breakthrough for Assad", The Guardian, 5 June 2013. Available at: https://www.theguardian.com/world/2013/jun/05/syria-army-seizes-qusair

significantly after the Iranian regime established a continuous land corridor to Lebanon in 2003. The alliance between the Iranian and Assad regimes was also based on a shared religious identity. The Assad regime and family belong to the Alawite minority in Syria, which constitutes a maximum of 15% of the Syrian population. Alawites, an offshoot of Shia Islam, are doctrinally closer to Shi'ism than to Sunni Islam. Iran has key economic interests in Syria, including investments and trade relationships that it sought to protect.[71] The chaos of the Syrian Civil War put those interests at risk. So, the Tehran provided military and financial support for Assad for decades, thus ensuring the protection of its economic interests in Syria.[72]

---

[71] Dr Majid Rafizadeh, "Iran's economic stake in Syria", Foreign Policy, 4 January 2013. Available at:
https://foreignpolicy.com/2013/01/04/irans-economic-stake-in-syria/
[72] Navvar Saban, "Factbox: Iranian Influence and Presence in Syria, Atlantic Council, 5 November 2020. Available at:
https://www.atlanticcouncil.org/blogs/menasource/factbox-iranian-influence-and-presence-in-syria/

Bashar al-Assad meets the Iran regime's Supreme Leader Ayatollah Ali Khamenei after the death of Iranian regime President Ebrahim Raisi. In this moment, Assad and Khamenei appear in a cordial embrace, symbolizing an enduring strategic alignment. (Photo: Office of Iran regime's Supreme Leader)

The Iranian regime also saw the civil war in Syria[73] as an ideal way for them to embrace and mobilise foreign militias in the country, as it had done in Iraq. Once again, they relied on General Qassem Soleimani to wield authority in Syria, organizing and arming local militias, while integrating his own Iranian militias into Bashar al-Assad's military and security apparatus, granting them quasi-legal status within Syrian institutions. Iran's military presence in the country became so entrenched that they became an easy target for Israeli air strikes, forcing the Iranian

---

73 For detailed examination of the Iranian regime's effort to save the Assad regime see "How Iran Fuels Syria War," The National Council of Resistance of Iran, U.S. Representative Office, 15 November 2015. Available at: https://www.amazon.com/How-Iran-Fuels-Syria-War/dp/1944942904

regime to seek a more effective way of concealing and defending its forces. This led to the formation of the Local Defence Forces (LDF), modelled on the Popular Mobilization Forces (PMF) in Iraq. LDF units were embedded within specific brigades of the Syrian army and even within quasi-state private security firms.

The Iranian regime encouraged Syria's Alawite minority to create special militias, even recruiting Sunnis, especially from some Sunni tribes, in Aleppo, Raqqa and Deir Ezzor. Militias were sometimes recruited for religious reasons and mobilized to defend shrines deemed sacred to the Shi'ite community. This was especially evident in the Sayyida Zainab district of Damascus, which was home to the holy shrines of Shi'ites. Those who were recruited into these militias received up to 45 days of basic weapons training, with some undergoing up to six months of heavy weapons instruction.

The formation of the National Defence Forces (NDF) commenced in 2012 in the city of Homs, under the strict guidance and control of the Iranians. The NDF included members from all sects, such as Sunnis, Alawites and Druze, with headquarters in each of the Syrian provinces. The NDF was the largest of the militias in Syria and reportedly had 40,000 fighters by 2015, though estimates vary, while the LDF grew to over 50,000 by 2018.[74] The Iranian mullahs demanded the NDF's formal integration into Syria's military structure, mirroring the legitimization of Iraq's PMF.

Assad disbanded the National Defence Forces in 2016, compelling Tehran to redirect its recruitment efforts toward fighters from Aleppo, Deir Ezzor, and Raqqa provinces, who were integrated into the Syrian army.

The Iranian regime deployed various tactics to recruit members of the LDF, including the pretext of requiring fighters to protect Shi'ite shrines. However, primary recruitment incentive was financial compensation. Every fighter in the Fatemiyoun brigade was given from $450 to $700 monthly, a significant salary in the Middle East.

The Fatemiyoun brigade was composed largely of Afghan-Shi'ite fighters recruited in Iran[75]. Other militias reportedly received $200–$300 per month, sourced from the IRGC's estimated $7.6 billion annual budget. These recruits were routinely sent to IRGC training camps in Mashhad in northeastern Iran, before returning to Syria by air or through Iraq.

---

[74] Orit Perlov and Udi Dekel, "The Model of Iranian Influence in Syria," INSS Insight No. 1079, 27 July 2018
[75] Phillip Smyth, "Iran's Afghan Shiite Fighters in Syria", The Washington Institute for Near East Policy, 3 June 2014.
Available at: https://www.washingtoninstitute.org/policy-analysis/irans-afghan-shiite-fighters-syria

Hezbollah also maintained a strong presence in Syria, with an estimated 5,000 to 8,000 Lebanese fighters present at any given time.

However, as military activity in the civil war decreased, Iran sought new ways of infiltrating Syrian society, by deepening economic ties and developing strong links with Syrian businessmen. Private security companies were also prevalent and allowed to operate legally in Syria under Assad. Iran exploited these security companies to extend their influence and penetrating sensitive sectors and securing key logistical corridors such as the Baghdad–Damascus highway.

The Iranian regime significantly expanded its economic activity, infiltrating the local civil and business communities. It also intensively engaged in charitable initiatives through organizations such as the Jihad al-Bina Organisation, which focused on restoring schools and health centres. Iranian cultural centres also played a key role in disseminating Iranian cultural narratives and regime-aligned messaging throughout Syrian society, ensuring that there was a distinctive Iranian presence in Syria for many years.

Empire's Collapse: Assad's Fall and Iran's Reckoning

On 8 December 2024, the Baathist regime led by President Bashar al-Assad collapsed during a major offensive by opposition forces. The offensive was spearheaded by Tahrir al-Sham (HTS) and supported mainly by the Turkish-backed Syrian National Army amid the ongoing civil war that began in 2011. The capture of Damascus, after only eleven days, marked the end of the Assad family's tyrannical rule, which had governed Syria as a hereditary, totalitarian regime since Hafez al-Assad, Bashar's father, assumed power in 1971 following the 'Corrective Movement', a bloodless coup d'état led by General Hafez al-Assad on 13 November 1970 in Syria.

As the rebel coalition known as the Southern Operations Room, advanced towards Damascus, Bashar al-Assad departed Syria by air to Russia, where he joined his family, already in exile, and was granted asylum by Vladimir Putin.[4] Following Assad's departure, opposition forces declared victory on state television. Concurrently, the Russian Ministry of Foreign Affairs confirmed Assad's resignation and his departure from Syria.[5][6]

The swift fall of the Assad regime was met with shock and surprise throughout the world. Syrian opposition fighters were themselves reportedly surprised at how quickly the Syrian government collapsed in the wake of their offensive.[7] The collapse of Assad's regime was not solely the result of Iran's strategic overreach, but also reflected broader structural weaknesses within the Syrian state, internal discontent, and the exhaustion of a fragmented society ravaged by years of civil war .

Analysts consider this incident the biggest blow to the Iranian regime and regional strategy, and the biggest blow to the regime's existence. Tehran's failure to preserve the Assad regime—despite an estimated $50 billion investment and the loss of thousands of IRGC personnel—has significantly undermined its credibility among regional allies.

Post-Assad, Iran is seeking to maintain influence through allies like the Houthi rebels in Yemen and Iraqi militias, though U.S. airstrikes on Houthis, ordered by President Trump in March 2025 to counter Red Sea attacks, hold Iran accountable.[76] Iran's response remains uncertain amid regional shifts.[77]

This will certainly backfire with the Trump administration. The Saudis, who view Iran as a competitor, will also see Assad's fall as an opportunity to reduce Iranian influence and potentially support a

---

[76] "How US strikes against Yemen's Houthis have unfolded," *Reuters*, 28 April 2025. Available at: https://www.reuters.com/world/us-campaign-against-yemens-houthis-2025-04-28/

[77] Renad Mansour, Hayder Al-Shakeri, Haid Haid. "The Shape-Shifting 'Axis of Resistance." Chatham House, March 2025. Available at: https://www.chathamhouse.org/sites/default/files/2025-03/2025-03-06-shape-shifting-axis-resistance-mansour-shakeri-haid.pdf

new Syrian leadership that aligns more closely with Gulf interests.

The fall of the Assad regime in Syria has certainly created a new geopolitical landscape that will potentially affect the relationship between Russia and Iran, who have historically aligned in the Middle East due to shared strategic interests, particularly in their desire to limit U.S. influence in the region. This foundational aspect might encourage them to continue cooperating even after the fall of the Assad regime. However, Vladimir Putin's ongoing difficulties in his illegal war in Ukraine have put further strains on this relationship. Both countries were involved in Syria primarily to ensure their interests in the Middle East were secured, such as maintaining a critical ally, protecting their military investments (like Russia's naval facility in Tartus), and countering extremist groups.

But in the post-Assad scenario, dynamics will inevitably shift more towards competition. Both countries have different visions for Syria's future. Russia and Iran now compete for influence over Syria's reconstruction. Iran's influence in Syria has been primarily through supporting Shi'ite militias and establishing a corridor for influence stretching to Lebanon (via Hezbollah), while Russia's more state-centric approach has aimed at stabilizing a central Syrian government. They might both now vie for influence over the new government or key entities in the region. On January 17, 2025, Iranian President Masoud Pezeshkian and Russian President Vladimir Putin signed a 20-year strategic partnership treaty in Moscow to deepen cooperation, amid Syria's collapse.[78]

While Tehran may redouble its efforts to maintain influence through militia networks and opportunistic diplomacy, its strategic failure in Syria has dealt a significant blow to the credibility and cohesion of the velāyat-e faqih's regional ambitions. No amount of propaganda can disguise the reality: Iran's ability to control regional events is diminishing sharply, and even its allies are beginning to hedge their bets.

The aftermath is not merely a geopolitical defeat, it is a public unravelling of Iran's myth of unstoppable influence in the Middle East. The fall of Assad is not just the collapse of a dictator, it is the beginning of the end for Iran's imperial ambitions.

---

[78] Isachenkov, Vladimir. "Russia and Iran Sign a Partnership Treaty to Deepen Their Ties in the Face of Western Sanctions." *AP News*, 17 January 2025. Available at: https://apnews.com/article/russia-putin-iran-pezeshkian-treaty-partnership-71a20990373851741d1fe76a81699036

9

"When the elephants fight, it is the grass that suffers."
- *African proverb*

THE IRANIAN REGIME'S SUPPORT FOR THE HOUTHI REBELS IN YEMEN

Proxy Power: Iran's Houthi Gambit

The Iranian regime's support for the Houthi rebels in Yemen is rooted in its broader regional strategy and a complex interplay of domestic and geopolitical considerations. Yemen is important to the Iranian regime in several ways. Control over the Red Sea and the Bab al-Mandeb Strait, alongside influence along Saudi Arabia's southern border, are central to this strategy. In the regime's regional strategy, Saudi Arabia plays a very special and perhaps the most important role. Khomeini, followed by Khamenei, who claims to be the leader of the Islamic world, cannot give up Mecca and Medina (the two holy shrines), the largest and most important centres of Islam in Saudi Arabia. For this reason, Khomeini wrote in his will: "If we pass over Saddam Hussein, we will not pass over King Fahd (who was the king of Saudi Arabia at that time) (Khomeini's will).

The regime has employed several tactics to pressure Saudi Arabia: (1) inciting unrest among the country's Shi'ite minority (which constitutes roughly 20% of the population); (2) threatening to close the Strait of Hormuz or engaging in maritime piracy in the Persian Gulf; and (3) seeking hegemony over the Bab al-Mandeb Strait to impose a quasi-naval blockade.

The Houthi clan provides an opportunity for Iran to implement this strategy. The Houthis are part of the followers of the Zaydiyyah sect, which is considered a branch of Shi'ite Islam, and they believe in the five Imams, unlike the Shi'ites of Iran, Iraq and Lebanon. Zaydis make up about 40 percent of Yemen's population, and the Houthis make up 10 to 15 percent. The Iranian regime has organized the Ansarullah movement from among the Houthis with a calculated Hezbollah-style plan.

Iran and Saudi Arabia are regional rivals, often supporting opposing sides in conflicts throughout the Middle East. Saudi Arabia views the Houthis as an Iranian proxy aiming to undermine its influence. By backing the Houthis, Iran sees an opportunity to challenge Saudi dominance and potentially drain its resources. Iran's support also functions as a bargaining chip in its broader geopolitical strategy. By having influence over the Houthis, Iran can leverage this position in negotiations related to other regional issues, potentially including its nuclear programme and sanctions relief.

Supporting the Houthis allows Iran to promote its narrative and project solidarity with Shi'ite groups across the region. Through the IRGC and its extra-territorial Quds Force, Iran supplies the Houthis with arms, including missiles and drones. Iran has also trained Houthi fighters both in Yemen and abroad, and in some cases has used Lebanese Hezbollah as their trainer and organizer The support has enabled the Houthis to sustain their military campaign, prolonging the war and worsening the humanitarian crisis in Yemen. The conflict has led to severe humanitarian consequences, with thousands of civilians killed, millions displaced, and widespread famine and disease. The continuing struggle has impeded efforts for relief and reconstruction.

Chaos and Costs: Yemen's War and Regional Ruin:

The flow of arms and the ongoing warfare have created a state of instability that threatens neighbouring countries and overall regional security. It has also led to maritime security threats in the Red Sea and Bab el-Mandeb shipping routes, disrupting global maritime commerce and raising shipping costs worldwide.

The complexity of the conflict has also drawn in other international actors. The U.S. and other Western allies have shown involvement through military support for Saudi Arabia and condemnation of Iranian actions, affecting global diplomatic relations. The ongoing support has skewed Yemen's political landscape, reducing the prospects for a unified and stable government. Various factions, including the internationally recognised government and southern separatists, continue to vie for power amidst the fragmentation exacerbated by sustained external interference.

The Houthis have been supplied with kamikaze drones and missiles by Iran, with IRGC trainers developing their attack skills, heavily deployed in deadly assaults on commercial shipping in the Red Sea and Gulf of Aden, seriously disrupting world trade. Claiming to defend their Palestinian brothers, the Houthis have launched missile attacks on Israel itself. Meanwhile, the U.S. Navy's efforts at stopping the attacks on shipping have led to the most sustained combat engagement for U.S. sailors since World War II, though these efforts have failed to halt the attacks.

In March 2025, President Trump ordered sustained U.S. airstrikes on Houthi targets in Yemen to counter their attacks on Red Sea shipping, warning

Iran to halt support, as reported by Reuters.[79] The Houthis currently rule a third of Yemen's territory and two-thirds of its population.

Yemen's civil war continues today, with its front lines largely frozen. The Houthi government, based in the capital, Sanaa, is recognised only by Iran. Influenced by strict readings of Islamic law and local caste-based traditions, Houthi governance is considered repressive by human rights watchdogs. The Houthis' Iranian-inspired slogan highlights their ambitions beyond Yemen: "God is great, death to America, death to Israel, a curse upon the Jews, victory to Islam." The United States designates them as a terrorist group.

Iran is the Houthis' primary benefactor, providing them mostly with security assistance, such as weapons transfers, training, and intelligence support. In late January 2024, for example, U.S. forces intercepted a shipment carrying military aid from Iran to the Houthis, including drone parts, missile warheads, and anti-tank missile units. Such aid mainly reaches the Houthis via Iran's IRGC.

In return for Iran's aid, the Houthis serve as an increasingly important part of Iran's "axis of

---

[79] Reuters News Agency, "Trump Vows to Hold Iran Responsible for Houthi Attacks." Reuters, 17 March 2025. Available at: https://www.reuters.com/world/middle-east/us-piles-pressure-yemens-houthis-with-new-airstrikes-2025-03-17/

resistance," a network of state and nonstate actors seeking to undermine Western influence in the Middle East. The stated mission includes expelling U.S. forces from the region, dismantling the Israeli state, and coercing regional actors aligned with Western powers. In addition, IRGC and Hezbollah representatives advise the Houthis' military command authority, the Jihad Council.

For the Houthis, the Iran connection provides more sophisticated weaponry than they could acquire on their own, especially missiles and drones. Iranian assistance has significantly enhanced the Houthis' combat capabilities, enabling them to sustain battlefield superiority against rival Yemeni factions.

Global Flashpoint: Houthi Attacks and Iran's Isolation

In what the Houthis claim is an expression of solidarity with Hamas and the Palestinian cause, the group has targeted vessels allegedly linked to the United States and Israel in the Red Sea, and even fired missiles at Israel, with ruinous impacts for international shipping. Tehran has voiced its unequivocal support for the operations and reportedly assists the Houthis in targeting vessels.

Since the start of the Israel Hamas war on 7th October 2023, the Iranian-backed Houthis have stepped up their drone and missile attacks on cargo vessels in the Red Sea, forcing major firms to take the longer, costlier route around the southern tip of Africa. According to the Pentagon, the Houthis have launched more than 100 such attacks,[80] targeting shipping from at least 35 different countries, with IRGC trainers enhancing their capabilities. The Houthis have been trained and armed by the IRGC. Kamikaze drones manufactured in Iran have been used in the attacks.

The Pentagon also claimed the Iranians were behind a 23rd December 2023 drone attack on the MV Pluto ship, a chemical tanker flying the Liberian flag and operated by a Dutch entity[81]. The ship is owned by a Japanese company. The drone, which according to the Pentagon was fired from Iran, exploded above the tanker in the Indian Ocean, 200 nautical miles off the Indian coast, causing a fire and some damage, although no casualties were reported. In December 2023, IRGC official Mohammad Reza Naqdi warned that Iran could disrupt major sea routes if Israel's war with Hamas continued, according to Tasnim news

---

[80] Eleanor Watson, "U.S. warships and aircraft strike over a dozen Houthi targets in Yemen", CBS News, 4 October 2024. Available at: https://www.cbsnews.com/news/us-airstrikes-yemen-iran-backed-houthi-rebels/
[81] "Pentagon says Iranian drone 'attack' hit chemical tanker near India", Reuters, 23 December 2023. Available at: https://www.reuters.com/world/pentagon-says-iranian-drone-attack-hit-chemical-tanker-near-india-2023-12-24/

agency.[82] "With the continuation of these crimes, America and its allies should expect the emergence of new resistance forces and the closure of other waterways," he said.

In response to the growing threat, the U.S. warship USS Laboon intercepted four kamikaze drones fired from Yemen by the Houthis. Another drone narrowly missed a Norwegian-flagged tanker, and one more struck the MV Saibaba, an Indian-flagged tanker in the Red Sea, in the run-up to Christmas 2023. The Biden administration accused Tehran of being "deeply involved" in planning the attacks, claiming that its intelligence was a critical factor enabling the Houthis to target commercial shipping in the Red Sea.

More than 20 countries have joined a US-led multinational Red Sea coalition aimed at safeguarding international maritime commerce in the region. Major General Pat Ryder, a Pentagon spokesman, said the Houthis were "attacking the economic wellbeing and prosperity of nations around the world," effectively becoming "bandits along the international highway that is the Red Sea."[83] He said that the

---

[82] Struan Stevenson, "Have Iran's Mullahs Reached a Tipping Point With West Over Their Attacks on Commercial Shipping?" Townhall, 2 January 2024. Available at:
https://townhall.com/columnists/struanstevenson/2024/01/02/have-irans-mullahs-reached-a-tipping-point-with-west-over-their-attacks-on-commercial-shipping-n2633078
[83] "More than 20 countries join US-led coalition to protect Red Sea shipping", France 24, 22 December 2023. Available at:

coalition forces will "serve as a highway patrol of sorts, patrolling the Red Sea and the Gulf of Aden to respond to, and assist as necessary, commercial vessels that are transiting this vital international waterway".

This Pentagon move caused panic in Tehran and in response to U.S. actions, Iran's Foreign Minister Abbas Araghchi claimed the Houthis act independently, stating Tehran does not dictate their actions, per Reuters (2024). The denials had a hollow ring, however, given the fiery rhetoric expressed routinely during Friday prayers in the Islamic Republic, where IRGC commanders have cried "Death to America" and "Death to Israel".

Nevertheless, in March 2025, President Trump stated that henceforth he intended to hold Tehran directly responsible for any Houthi missile or drone attacks on commercial shipping in the Gulf. His warning coincided with a sustained U.S. air and bombing assault on Houthi positions in Yemen.

UNICEF reports 2.2 million Yemeni children face malnutrition due to the war, exacerbated by Houthi blockades and Iranian-backed escalation.[84] In return, Tehran has gained a strategic outpost on the

---

https://www.france24.com/en/middle-east/20231222-more-than-20-countries-join-us-led-coalition-to-protect-red-sea-shipping

[84] UNICEF. "Nutrition." UNICEF Yemen, 2024. Available at: https://www.unicef.org/yemen/nutrition

doorstep of its chief rival, Saudi Arabia, and a powerful lever in negotiations with the West.

Yet, this policy has begun to backfire. The international community, led by the United States, has increasingly come to regard the Iranian regime as directly culpable for Houthi aggression. The mullahs' hollow denials ring even more implausible in the face of overwhelming evidence linking Tehran to attacks on international shipping and regional destabilisation. As the U.S. and its allies move to confront this threat more forcefully, the Iranian regime now faces not only mounting diplomatic isolation but the possibility of direct military escalation it may no longer be equipped to contain. The strategy that once gave Iran influence on the cheap is now threatening to bring serious costs, diplomatically, militarily, and economically, further undermining the regime's credibility at home and abroad.

10

"Fanaticism is overcompensation for doubt."
- *Robert Frost*

THE GENESIS OF HEZBOLLAH IN LEBANON

Birth of a Proxy: Iran's Creation of Hezbollah

Hezbollah has been one of the most sinister products of Ayatollah Khomeini and the religious dictatorship in Iran, and the regime's principal instrument for exporting its ideological vision, including the aspiration for an Islamic world government.

The instability resulting from Lebanon's civil war (1975-1990) provided fertile ground for the emergence of militant groups. Iran sought to expand its influence in the region by supporting a Shi'ite faction within this milieu.

Khomeini organized Hezbollah in 1982 in the midst of the Lebanese civil war and delegated oversight to then-President Khamenei. In an interview on September 23, 2010, Hassan Nasrallah said: In 1982, it was decided to form "a large group, and thus nine people were elected on behalf of the brothers who supported the Resistance, including Seyyed Abbas

Mousavi. Naturally, I was not among these nine people, because I was young at the time and was about 22 or 23 years old".

The nine individuals met with Imam Khomeini. Addressing Imam Khomeini, they said, "We believe in your Imamate, Wilayat [guardianship], and leadership. What is our duty?" In response, Imam Khomeini emphasized that it is your duty to resist and stand against the enemy with all our might, even if your resources are limited and your numbers are small.

"Thus, the meeting during which our brothers came to the presence of the Imam laid the foundation stone for the formation of the Islamic Resistance Front under the blessed name of "Hezbollah" in Lebanon. At that time, our brothers told the Imam, "We cannot constantly disturb you about various issues. Therefore, we ask you to nominate a representative on your behalf so that we can refer to him on various issues." He then introduced Imam Khamenei, who was the president at the time, and said, "Mr. Khamenei is my representative." Accordingly, relations between the Lebanese Hezbollah and Ayatollah Khamenei began from the very first hours of the establishment of this group."[85]

---

[85] "From the First Contact of the Hezbollah Party in Lebanon with the Leader of the Revolution to a Memory Told by Imam Khomeini" (in Farsi). *Hawzah News Agency*, 23 September 2019. Available at:

Over time, Hezbollah became a political actor in Lebanon, a move that further strengthened it, supporting Hezbollah both as a tool to expand Iran's strategic reach and as a deterrent against U.S. and Israeli actions. Post-1982, Syria became an essential conduit for logistical and military support to Hezbollah. Iran's IRGC played a crucial role in creating and arming Hezbollah. The IRGC trained Hezbollah militias in guerrilla warfare, intelligence, and tactical skills. Iran supplied Hezbollah with arms, including rockets and missiles, enhancing its military capability to engage in prolonged asymmetric warfare.

Power and Peril: Hezbollah's Rise and Regional Impact

Over time, Hezbollah evolved into what many military analysts describe as a medium-sized standing army. By 2016, Western intelligence assessments estimated Hezbollah's fighting strength at over 20,000 active fighters, with another 25,000 reservists. Its arsenal included an estimated 150,000 rockets and missiles, some with ranges capable of striking deep into Israeli territory. Hezbollah's battlefield experience, particularly in Syria alongside Assad's forces, further professionalised its units, allowing it to operate at a level far exceeding that of a typical non-state actor.

از-اولین-ارتباط-حزب-/https://www.hawzahnews.com/news/865054
از-ای-خاطره-تا-انقلاب-رهبر-با-لبنان-الله

Iran also provided significant financial support, establishing a steady flow of resources that allowed Hezbollah to build social services, media outlets, and a political apparatus alongside its military wing.

Hezbollah's military power was put on display during its 2006 war with Israel, showcasing its ability to inflict damage. Above all, Hezbollah's position on Israel's border proved that Iran's strategy could deter attacks in and around Iran. This period was also the apogee of Iran's and Hezbollah's soft-power support across the Middle East, which Tehran is eager to recover in the current crisis.

Hezbollah's prominence in the Arab world, however, began to wane following its controversial intervention in the Syrian civil war. The group's support for Bashar al-Assad's brutal suppression of predominantly Sunni protesters alienated large segments of the Arab public. Once seen as a heroic resistance movement against Israeli aggression, Hezbollah came to be viewed increasingly as an instrument of sectarian repression, tarnishing the image Iran had worked so hard to cultivate across the region.

The 2006 conflict between Hezbollah and Israel resulted in significant destruction in Lebanon and loss of life, but also increased Hezbollah's stature in the Arab world as a resistance movement. Hezbollah's intervention in the Syrian Civil War on behalf of the Assad regime further demonstrated its strategic importance to Iran and its role as a regional military actor. Iran's backing of Hezbollah has contributed to its characterization by Western and some regional actors as a state sponsor of terrorism. While designated a terrorist group by the U.S., the EU labels only Hezbollah's military wing as such, reflecting debates over its political legitimacy. Support for Hezbollah has resulted in economic sanctions and diplomatic isolation for Iran and complexities in international relations concerning peace and stability in the Middle East. Iran provided Hezbollah $700 million annually, per U.S. Treasury reports (2023), equipping it with 150,000 rockets by 2024.

Over time, Hezbollah grew stronger, and the Iranian regime became more reliant on it. The influential Quds force commander, Qassem Soleimani, was the key architect and manager of Iran's 'axis of resistance'. Since his death, Tehran came to depend more on Hezbollah to manage and coordinate unity among its proxies. During the Syrian war, Hezbollah played an instrumental role alongside Iran in supporting Syria's president, Bashar al-Assad. Despite criticism from regional actors, including Hamas, for their part in suppressing a popular uprising and the decade-long massacre and displacement of Syrians, they succeeded in setting up militias and positioning in the Golan area, creating another dangerous front on Israel's border.

By the early 2000s, Hezbollah emerged not only as a formidable militia but also as a significant political entity in Lebanon, influencing the nation's politics. Hezbollah's transformation from a purely militant resistance group into a dominant political actor in Lebanon began with its formal entry into Lebanese politics in the early 1990s, following the Taif Agreement. By participating in parliamentary elections and forming alliances with secular and Christian parties, Hezbollah strategically embedded itself within the Lebanese political system while maintaining its military autonomy.[86]

Nevertheless, Hezbollah's participation in Lebanese politics did little to resolve the fundamental tensions created by its dual identity as both a militia and a political party. The organisation's refusal to disarm, despite the provisions of the Taif Agreement and subsequent UN resolutions, created a perpetual source of instability within Lebanon's fragile sectarian balance. For many Lebanese citizens, Hezbollah's military autonomy became synonymous with lawlessness, undermining both the credibility of the Lebanese state and efforts at national sovereignty.

Hezbollah built extensive social programmes in health, education, and housing, garnering substantial support from the Shi'ite community in Lebanon.

---

[86] Norton, Augustus Richard. *Hezbollah: A Short History*. 3rd ed. Princeton: Princeton University Press, 2007.

Hezbollah's 2022 election of 13 parliamentary seats and extensive welfare programs, like schools and hospitals, cemented its dual role as a militia and political force.

Nevertheless, Hezbollah's deep entrenchment in Lebanese politics has failed to insulate it from the country's mounting economic collapse. Hezbollah's perceived prioritisation of Iran's strategic interests over Lebanon's national wellbeing has become an increasingly salient grievance. Its interventionist policies, particularly its entanglement in conflicts beyond Lebanon's borders, have diverted resources away from domestic needs. Critics argue that Hezbollah's actions have exacerbated Lebanon's international isolation, deepened its economic despair, and compromised any prospect of coherent state governance. As Lebanon teeters on the brink of failed-state status, Hezbollah faces a credibility crisis that even its vast patronage networks may be unable to mitigate.

The devastation of Lebanon's banking sector, combined with international sanctions targeting Hezbollah's financial networks, has severely constrained its patronage system. Even among its Shi'ite support base, dissatisfaction has grown over the prioritisation of Hezbollah's regional military adventures over domestic wellbeing. Increasing numbers of Lebanese, across all sects, blame

Hezbollah for perpetuating corruption, stalling reforms, and dragging Lebanon deeper into isolation.

While Shi'ite communities view Hezbollah as a protector, Sunni and Christian Lebanese often resent its armed dominance, seeing it as an Iranian proxy. Although Hezbollah enjoys significant support within Lebanon's Shi'ite community, many Lebanese, particularly Sunnis, Christians, and Druze, view its militia status as undermining national sovereignty and dragging Lebanon into costly regional conflicts, notably the devastating 2006 war with Israel.

Crumbling Alliance: Nasrallah's Fall and Iran's Decline

The elimination of Hezbollah's leader Hassan Nasrallah in Beirut in September 2024, a seismic event, shattered his close friend and ally Ayatollah Ali Khamenei, Iran's Supreme Leader and Hezbollah's main sponsor. Nasrallah's successor, Hashem Safieddine, was also killed in an Israeli airstrike in Beirut before the funeral of his predecessor had even taken place.

On 25 August 2024, Israel launched a massive air attack on military targets in southern Lebanon, in what they described as a pre-emptive strike on Hezbollah. Hezbollah then launched hundreds of rockets aimed at military targets in northern Israel in retaliation for Israel's killing of one of their senior commanders, triggering fears that the exchange of fire could lead to all-out war. Iran responded to the targeted killings of Hamas leader Ismail Haniyeh in Tehran (31 July 2024) and Hezbollah leader Hassan Nasrallah in Beirut (21 September 2024) by launching over 200 ballistic missiles at Israel. The attack, however, caused only minimal destruction.

The then U.S. Secretary of State Antony Blinken repeatedly tried to broker an end to the Israel-Hamas war in Gaza that has claimed more than 50,000 Palestinian lives. Blinken met with Israel's President Isaac Herzog and Prime Minister Binyamin Netanyahu, describing his peace bid as "probably the best, maybe the last, opportunity to get the hostages home, to get a cease-fire and to put everyone on a better path to enduring peace and security."[87]

However, following the large-scale ballistic missile attack on Israel by Iran on 1 October 2024, calls for restraint from Washington became markedly more muted. The arrival of President Donald Trump in the White House led to a temporary ceasefire and the exchange of some Israeli hostages for hundreds of Hamas prisoners. Donald Trump controversially

---

[87] Antony Blinken, quoted in "Probably the best, maybe the last' chance to save Gaza hostages," Politico, 19 August 2024.
Available at: https://www.politico.eu/article/us-blinken-says-this-is-best-maybe-the-last-chance-to-get-hostages-out-of-gaza-and-secure-ceasefire/

announced that he wished to see all remaining Palestinians relocated from Gaza to "other" countries in the Middle East, while America re-built the destroyed Palestinian homeland into a "Gaza Riviera". His idea was universally condemned.

Iranian support for the creation of Hezbollah has had profound and far-reaching effects on regional geopolitics, Lebanon's domestic landscape, and international relations, embodying Iran's strategic aims but also fostering significant instability and conflict. Ayatollah Ali Khamenei was left shaken by the assassination in Beirut of his close friend and ally-in-chief Hassan Nasrallah, the head of Hezbollah on 27 September 2024. Nasrallah's death deeply affected the 85-year-old Supreme Leader. Khamenei's rare public mourning of Nasrallah, calling him 'my brother' in a 2024 speech, underscored the personal and strategic blow of his death.

The creation and evolution of Hezbollah as Iran's most successful proxy force exemplify the Islamic Republic's long-term strategy of exporting its revolutionary ideology through militancy and manipulation. What began as a response to Israel's occupation of southern Lebanon transformed into a full-fledged extension of Tehran's foreign policy apparatus, militarily sophisticated, politically embedded, and ideologically loyal.

Iran's investment in Hezbollah not only gave it a potent weapon on Israel's doorstep, but also deeply destabilised Lebanon's internal politics and compromised its sovereignty. Hezbollah's dual role as both a political actor and a paramilitary force ensured that Lebanon would remain tethered to Iran's regional ambitions, often at the expense of its own national interest and democratic development.

For Ayatollah Khamenei, the loss of Nasrallah is more than symbolic, it signals the crumbling of a decades-long project to dominate the Middle East through terror and ideological warfare. With mounting pressure from international coalitions and internal resistance movements, the era of unchecked Iranian expansion may finally be entering its twilight.

In the wider context, Hezbollah's setbacks reflect the broader erosion of Iran's regional influence, as economic crises, military losses, and political isolation steadily erode the foundations of the so-called "axis of resistance."

Tehran's long-standing strategy of asymmetric warfare, waged through disciplined proxies like Hezbollah, relies upon the credibility and effectiveness of these groups. The erosion of Hezbollah's standing, both militarily and politically, not only weakens Iran's leverage against Israel but also undermines the ideological claim that the Islamic Republic remains the vanguard of anti-Western resistance. In this sense, Hezbollah's trajectory serves as a bellwether for the broader fortunes of Iranian expansionism across the Middle East.

11

"Terrorism is the war of the poor, and war is the terrorism of the rich."
- Peter Ustinov

TERRORISM AND HOSTAGE TAKING AS IRANIAN STATE POLICY

Since its inception in 1979, the Iranian regime has pursued terrorism not merely as a tool, but as a foundational pillar of its foreign policy. Ayatollah Khomeini's theocracy quickly discovered the value of assassination, hostage-taking, and proxy warfare to project power, silence dissent, and coerce foreign governments. These tactics have remained central to Iran's strategy for more than four decades.

1980s–1990s: Establishing the Terror Template

The regime's first major act of terrorism and hostage-taking was the occupation of the U.S. Embassy in Tehran on 4 November 1979, during which 52 American diplomats were held hostage for 444 days. Eight months after the revolution, the Iranian people's demands for democracy and political freedoms were becoming increasingly vocal. Democratic forces such as the People's Mojahedin Organization of Iran (PMOI) had begun to regain influence, particularly among the youth. Khomeini orchestrated the embassy seizure to suppress the rising tide of pro-democracy sentiment, exploiting widespread anti-American fervor to distract and consolidate power.

On the sixth anniversary of the hostage-taking of the U.S. Embassy, then Chief Justice Ayatollah Abdul-Karim Mousavi Ardebili told regime supporters at the embassy site that the 1979 takeover brought "the isolation of the liberals and the confusion of left-wing groups and the PMOI."[88]

The regime's other major act of international terrorism came on 23 October 1983, with the bombing of the U.S. Marine barracks in Beirut, killing 241 American servicemen and 58 French paratroopers. The attack, carried out by Hezbollah, founded in 1982 with IRGC training and funding, marked the formal beginning of Tehran's proxy war strategy.[89]

---

[88] Then-Chief Justice Ayatollah Abdul-Karim Mousavi Ardebili, Tehran Friday Congregation, 4 November 1985. Available at: https://mojahedin.org/links/books/democracy_betrayed.pdf
[89] U.S. Department of Defense. Report on the Bombing of the U.S. Marine Barracks in Beirut, 23 October 1983. Washington, D.C.: U.S. Department of Defense, 2003.

Throughout the late 1980s and 1990s, Iran extended its terror operations into Europe. In July 1989, Iranian agents murdered Abdol-Rahman Ghassemlou, leader of the Kurdish Democratic Party of Iran, during peace negotiations in Vienna.[90] In April 1990, Dr Kazem Rajavi, a leading human rights advocate and brother of NCRI leader Massoud Rajavi, was gunned down near Geneva by a team of Iranian operatives carrying diplomatic passports.[91]

Further assassinations followed: Shapour Bakhtiar, the Shah's last Prime Minister, was killed in Paris in August 1991; Dr Sadegh Sharafkandi and three of his colleagues were murdered in the Mykonos restaurant in Berlin in September 1992. The landmark Berlin court ruling in 1997 directly accused Iran's leadership, including Supreme Leader Khamenei, and President Rafsanjani, as well as its foreign minister and intelligence minister.[92]

Beyond Europe, Iran's reach extended to Latin America. The 1992 bombing of the Israeli embassy in Buenos Aires, killing 29, and the 1994 AMIA Jewish

---

[90] "The Murder of Kurdish Leader Abdol-Rahman Ghassemlou." *BBC News*, 13 July 2015.
[91] Case Report on the Assassination of Dr. Kazem Rajavi, 1997. Geneva: Swiss Federal Court Archives, 1997.
[92] "Judgment in the Mykonos Case, 10 November 1997." Berlin: Berlin State Court Archives, 1997.

community centre bombing, killing 85, were linked to Hezbollah and Iranian diplomatic channels.[93]

Iran also weaponised hostage-taking from the earliest days of the regime. The 444-day U.S. Embassy crisis in Tehran in 1979 provided Tehran with a model for using kidnapped foreigners to extract concessions, a tactic that quickly became a permanent fixture of its foreign policy arsenal.

1990s: Expanding Terror Operations Globally

In 1996, a devastating attack in Saudi Arabia further exposed Iran's direct involvement in international terrorism. The Khobar Towers bombing killed 19 U.S. servicemen and wounded hundreds. The FBI investigation traced the plot to Hezbollah Al-Hejaz, a group directly supported by Iran's IRGC and MOIS.[94] U.S. federal indictments in 2001 named Iranian officials as co-conspirators, but Tehran denied involvement.

---

[93] Argentine National Commission for the Investigation of the AMIA Bombing Final Report on the AMIA Bombing Investigation, Buenos Aires, 1999.
[94] Federal Bureau of Investigation Investigation Report on the Khobar Towers Bombing, 2001. Washington, D.C.: FBI Archives, 2001.

2000s: Expansion to Proxy Groups and Hostage Diplomacy

By the early 2000s, Iran had systematically expanded its proxy network beyond Hezbollah. It supported groups like Kata'ib Hezbollah and Asa'ib Ahl al-Haq in Iraq, the Houthis in Yemen, and Palestinian Islamic Jihad in Gaza, tailoring each relationship to the local political landscape. Each proxy served the regime's strategic objective: to extend Tehran's influence while maintaining plausible deniability.

The regime also refined its hostage-taking strategy, targeting dual nationals—academics, journalists, aid workers—accusing them of espionage in order to use them as diplomatic leverage. Hostages became instruments of coercion, traded for financial relief, prisoner exchanges, or political concessions.

The human cost of Iran's hostage-taking is profound. Detainees like Nazanin Zaghari-Ratcliffe, held from 2016 to 2022, endured psychological torture and family separation, with ripple effects on their communities.[95]

---

[95] "Iran: The crime of holding Nazanin Zaghari-Ratcliffe hostage must not go unpunished." Amnesty International, 1 June 2022. Available at:
https://www.amnesty.org/en/documents/mde13/5609/2022/en/

Victims of Iran's terror attacks, such as the 1994 AMIA bombing survivors, face lifelong trauma and loss, while targeted dissidents' families live in constant fear of reprisals. These personal tragedies, multiplied across decades, underscore the regime's disregard for human dignity and fuel global outrage against its policies.

2010s–2020s: Major Plots Foiled, Hostage Exchanges, and Escalation

Mrs Maryam Rajavi addressing NCRI's Annual Free Iran Summit in Paris in June 2018. Attended by over 100,000 people the event was the target of an Iranian bomb plot involving the accredited Iranian diplomat Assadollah Assadi. (Photo: NCRI)

Iran's terrorist activities reached a new height in the 2010s. In 2011, American authorities disrupted a plot to assassinate the Saudi Ambassador to Washington, Adel al-Jubair. The plan, orchestrated by Iran's Quds

Force and involving Mexican cartel intermediaries, was exposed in a federal sting operation.[96]

100,000 Iranians join hundreds of international dignitaries at the Free Iran World Summit 2018 in Paris. (Photo: NCRI)

In 2012 and 2013, Iranian operatives were implicated in several foiled terror plots targeting Israeli and Jewish assets across Thailand, India, Georgia, and Kenya (U.S. State Department Country Reports on Terrorism, 2013).[97]

In 2018, European police foiled a plot to bomb an NCRI rally near Paris. Assadollah Assadi, an Iranian diplomat based in Vienna, masterminded the

---

[96] NBC News, "US ties Iran to plot to kill Saudi ambassador," 11 October 2011. Available at:
https://www.nbcnews.com/id/wbna44861178
[97] Country Reports on Terrorism 2013, April 2014. https://2009-2017.state.gov/j/ct/rls/crt/2013/

operation, and was later sentenced to 20 years in prison by a Belgian court.[98]

Assadollah Assadi, released in a prisoner-swap for a Belgian hostage, arrives in Tehran on 26 May 2023, and is greeted as a hero by senior officials with handshakes and bouquets. (Photo: Tasnim News Agency)

The regime's impunity was further highlighted in November 2023 when Alejo Vidal-Quadras, a former Vice President of the European Parliament, survived an assassination attempt linked to Tehran.[99]

---

[98] "Iran Diplomat Given 20 Years for Paris Bomb Plot," France 24, 4 February 2021. Available at: https://www.france24.com/en/live-news/20210204-iran-diplomat-given-20-years-for-paris-bomb-plot

[99] Adam Sage, "How Iran pays mafia hitmen to carry out assassinations in Europe," The Times, 27 May 2025. Available at: https://www.thetimes.co.uk/article/iran-mafia-assassinations-europe-sg2k833v9

Former European Parliament Vice President, Prof. Alejo Vidal-Quadras (Photo: NCRI)

In 2024, Dutch authorities disrupted an IRGC-linked plot to conduct cyberattacks on Amsterdam's financial district, aiming to destabilize European markets, as reported by the Netherlands' AIVD intelligence agency.[100]

Meanwhile, Iran's practice of hostage diplomacy intensified. In 2022, the UK paid a £400 million debt to Iran, shortly followed by the release of two British-Iranian detainees.[101] In 2024, Sweden released Hamid

---

[100] AIVD, Annual Report 2023 (The Hague: General Intelligence and Security Service, 2024).
[101] Wintour, Patrick. "Iran Has Not Received £400m Agreed by UK at Time of Zaghari-Ratcliffe Release." The Guardian, 27 April 2022. Available at:
https://www.theguardian.com/world/2022/apr/27/iran-not-received-400m-agreed-uk-nazanin-zaghari-ratcliffe-anooshehashoori-release

Noury, convicted for crimes against humanity, in exchange for Swedish hostages.[102]

Iran's hostage diplomacy persisted with the 2020 kidnapping of Jamshid Sharmahd, a U.S. resident Iranian dissident, who was executed in 2024 after a sham trial, with an autopsy revealing brutal mutilation, as reported by his family.[103] In late 2024, Italy secured the release of a dual-national aid worker by freeing an IRGC arms smuggler linked to attacks on U.S. troops, a swap criticized for rewarding Tehran's extortion (La Repubblica, 2024). These cases underscore the regime's use of hostages to silence dissent and evade justice.

Iran's embassies have facilitated terrorist plots, with IRGC Quds Force and MOIS using diplomatic cover in cases like the 2018 Paris NCRI plot, per European intelligence. (Europol, 2021)

Iran's Proxy Strategy: Context and Reach

Iran's use of proxies extends beyond Hezbollah. Kata'ib Hezbollah in Iraq, known for attacking U.S.

---

[102] Jordan, Dearbail. "Iranian Convicted of War Crimes Freed in Swedish Swap." BBC News, 15 June 2024. Available at: https://www.bbc.com/news/articles/czrr2kemjleo

[103] "Jamshid Sharmahd, Iranian-German Prisoner Who Lived in California, Executed in Iran over Disputed Terror Charges." CBS News, 28 October 2024. Available at: https://www.cbsnews.com/news/jamshid-sharmahd-executed-iran-lived-in-us-disputed-terror-charges/

personnel; the Houthis in Yemen, who threaten shipping in the Red Sea; and militias in Syria and Gaza, all reflect a coherent doctrine of indirect warfare (Council on Foreign Relations Report, 2022). Tehran provides financial, ideological, and logistical support while allowing proxies local autonomy, a tactic that maximizes Iranian influence while minimizing risks.

Iran's maritime terrorism, executed through the IRGC Navy and Houthi proxies, threatens global trade. Since 2023, IRGC-supplied Houthi forces have attacked over 80 commercial vessels in the Red Sea, using drones and missiles, disrupting 12% of global trade through the Suez Canal.[104]

The IRGC's own naval units have seized tankers in the Strait of Hormuz, including a 2024 incident involving a British-flagged vessel, escalating tensions with Western powers.[105] These operations reflect Tehran's strategy to leverage maritime choke points for geopolitical coercion.

By the late 2010s, Iran expanded its terrorism to include cyberattacks targeting critical infrastructure. IRGC-linked units attacked U.S. banks, Saudi oil

---

[104] "Houthi attacks on ships disrupt global trade," DW, 13cJanuary 2024. Available at: https://www.dw.com/en/houthi-attacks-on-ships-disrupt-global-trade/a-67967525

[105] "Vessel Seized in Strait of Hormuz Amid Iran Tensions, Shipping Firms Say." Reuters, 13 April 2024. Available at: https://www.cnbc.com/2024/04/13/vessel-seized-in-strait-of-hormuz-amid-iran-tensions-shipping-firms.html

facilities, and Western water utilities.[106] These hybrid warfare tactics complement Iran's physical terrorism, amplifying its strategic impact while evading direct accountability.

Despite its Shi'ite ideological roots, Iran has occasionally allied with Sunni groups, notably Hamas, when strategic needs outweighed sectarian divides. This pragmatic approach underscores Tehran's flexibility and long-term vision.[107]

The IRGC's Quds Force orchestrates this global terror network through a sophisticated infrastructure of training camps, clandestine financing via front companies, and diplomatic cover provided by Iran's embassies. The Iranian regime's reliance on terrorism is not the product of rogue actors but of institutional policy. Supreme Leaders Khomeini and Khamenei have presided over a political culture that views terror and hostage-taking as legitimate extensions of statecraft.

Far from being historical relics, these tactics have evolved alongside the regime's broader ambitions. Terrorism serves as a means of deterrence,

---

[106] "Iranian Offensive Cyberattack Capabilities, Report IF11406. Congressional Research Service, 2024. Available at: https://www.congress.gov/crs-product/IF11406
[107] Byman, Daniel L. "The Iranian Revolution and Its Legacy of Terrorism." Brookings Institution, 24 January 2019. Available at: https://www.brookings.edu/articles/the-iranian-revolution-and-its-legacy-of-terrorism/

intimidation, and strategic leverage. It is cost-effective, difficult to directly attribute, and has repeatedly delivered results without significant backlash.

Toward a Coherent Response

The international community must acknowledge that Iran's terrorism and hostage-taking are not anomalies, but deliberate policies rooted in the structure of its theocratic regime. Continued appeasement, whether through ransom payments, prisoner swaps, or diplomatic overtures, only encourages Tehran's aggression.

Advocates of diplomacy argue that engaging Iran, particularly through nuclear talks, could moderate its behaviour and prevent escalation, but decades of concessions have only strengthened Tehran's resolve to pursue terrorism unabated.

Firm measures are essential. These include the global designation of the IRGC as a terrorist organization, the closure of Iranian embassies used for clandestine operations, and the creation of binding international protocols against hostage diplomacy.

Until Iran is confronted with serious, coordinated consequences, it will persist in its criminal enterprise, imperilling regional stability, emboldening authoritarian regimes worldwide, and undermining the international rules-based order.

Precedents for such measures exist. The designation of al-Qaeda as a terrorist organization in 2001 crippled its financial networks, while targeted sanctions on North Korea's elite since 2006 disrupted its illicit activities (UN Security Council Resolutions, 2001, 2006).

Similarly, Canada's 2012 closure of Iran's embassy in Ottawa curtailed Tehran's intelligence operations, setting a model for broader action. Applying these strategies to the IRGC and Iran's diplomatic network would signal a decisive shift, forcing Tehran to reckon with the costs of its terror policies. In 2024 Canada followed the U.S. in designating the IRGC as a foreign terrorist organization.

Some nations have taken decisive action against Iran's terrorism. In 2018, Albania expelled Iran's ambassador and a diplomat for plotting attacks on PMOI events, citing national security.[108] In 2016, Bahrain dismantled an IRGC-linked terror cell planning bombings, recalling its ambassador from

---

[108] Daragahi, Borzou. "Iran Diplomats Expelled from Albania Plotted against Dissidents, Source Says." The Independent, 20 December 2018. Available at:
https://www.independent.co.uk/news/world/europe/iran-albania-diplomats-dissidents-mek-terrorism-trump-bolton-irgc-a8692876.html

Tehran.[109] These measures contrast with Western appeasement and demonstrate the efficacy of targeted disruptions. Emulating such actions, through IRGC designations, embassy closures, and sanctions, could curtail Tehran's terror networks.

Between 2022 and 2024, several NCRI centres in France, Germany, Sweden and the United Kingdom were targeted for terrorist acts. These terrorist attacks have been carried out by hired criminal gangs. The Netherlands Intelligence and Security Agency wrote in May 2025 that the criminal gangs that targeted Professor Vidal Quadras had taken orders from Tehran.

The world must choose: either dismantle Tehran's machinery of terror now, or watch as it poisons the global order, one hostage, one bomb, and one broken promise at a time.

---

[109] "Bahrain Says Dismantled 'Terror Cell Linked' To Iran." Radio Free Europe/Radio Liberty, 6 January 2016. Available at: https://www.rferl.org/a/bahrain-iran-terror-cell/27471944.html

12

"Trust but verify."
- *Ronald Reagan*

IRAN'S NUCLEAR PROGRAMME: A WEB OF DECEPTION

Deceptive Beginnings: Iran's Nuclear Ambitions Unveiled

"Insanity is doing the same thing over and over again and expecting different results." By that standard, Western dealings with Iran have bordered on the deranged. For more than four decades, successive governments have attempted to appease the mullahs, sending planeloads of cash, lifting sanctions, blacklisting the democratic opposition at Tehran's request, all in the naïve hope that the regime might one day reform. Yet the outcome has been entirely predictable: heightened repression at home, escalated terrorism abroad, and a nuclear programme steadily advancing under the cover of deception.

This failed policy began more than forty years ago. The first prominent example was the story that became known as the Iran-Contra affair in Iran.

Instead of a decisive approach to this criminal act, the United States turned to a secret deal with the Iranian regime. The deal, which later became a political and judicial scandal in the United States, was exposed a few years later in the Tower Commission report. It was as simple as giving the Iranian regime some weapons (including TOW missiles) and taking a stand against the People's Mojahedin Organization of Iran (PMOI/MEK) in exchange for the release of American hostages.

It was under these circumstances that in July 1985, Richard Murphy, the US Assistant Secretary of State for the Near East, without prior debate, read an impromptu statement. That was not to confuse the Iranian Mujahideen with the Afghan Mujahideen. Afghans are a liberation force, and the Iranian Mujahideen are extremist Marxists. As later revealed in the Tower Commission report, this statement was one of the prepayments for the release of the hostages.

From its inception, Iran's nuclear programme has been a weaponisation project. Iran's nuclear ambitions trace back even before the Islamic Revolution. Initiated under the Shah's regime in the 1950s with U.S. backing through the Atoms for Peace programme, Iran's nuclear development gained new urgency under the mullahs, not to meet energy needs, but as a strategic asset to preserve and export the revolutionary regime. After 1979, the nuclear effort shifted from a Western-oriented civilian project to a clandestine military programme, tightly controlled by the new regime's security apparatus.

In mid-2024, Rafael Grossi, Director General of the International Atomic Energy Agency (IAEA), reported that Iran had denied inspectors access for more than three years. Surveillance cameras had been dismantled. Uranium was being enriched to 60% purity, a hair's breadth from weapons-grade[1]. In January 2025, Iran disabled newly installed IAEA remote monitoring sensors at its Bushehr facility, further obstructing verification efforts.[2] Compounding this, IRGC cyber units launched a sophisticated attack on IAEA databases in February 2025, attempting to erase inspection records[3]. Tehran was clearly pressing the accelerator.

By mid-2025, reports from the IAEA and independent intelligence sources indicated that Iran's stockpile of uranium enriched to near-weapons-grade levels had become alarmingly substantial. In tandem with accelerated centrifuge development and the hardening of nuclear facilities against aerial attack, Tehran signalled that it had moved beyond merely gaining a "breakout" capability, instead edging towards actual nuclear weaponisation readiness, a distinction often deliberately blurred by the regime's rhetoric.

Western complacency stretches back decades. It was not simply complacency but active self-deception that fuelled the West's disastrous engagement policy. Despite repeated instances of Iranian non-compliance, obfuscation, and deception, successive European governments clung to the illusion that Tehran's nuclear ambitions could be contained through dialogue. The regime exploited these overtures, expanding its clandestine activities under the cover of diplomatic talks while simultaneously presenting moderate facades to Western audiences.

Clandestine Advances: Iran's Nuclear Deceptions Exposed

For the first time, in June 1991, the People's Mojahedin Organization of Iran (PMOI) unveiled the regime's nuclear facilities in Washington. In March 1992, Massoud Rajavi wrote to UN Secretary-General Boutros Boutros-Ghali, informing him that the Iranian regime was "making extensive efforts to acquire nuclear weapons."

It was only in August 2002, when the NCRI uncovered secret nuclear facilities at Natanz and Arak, that the world began to pay attention. By then, European powers had continued to cooperate technically with Tehran, and Western intelligence agencies had not only failed to discover the true scope of the program, but also ignored the revelations of the resistance.

It was after this revelation that President Bush, the U.S. Vice President, Secretary of State, and other

American officials repeatedly emphasized that it was Iranian dissidents who exposed the regime's nuclear plans.

A confidential French report in 2003 warned that the regime was dangerously close to acquiring bomb-grade material. But rather than sounding the alarm, European policymakers chose the path of engagement, soft diplomacy that provided Tehran with time and legitimacy, while undermining opponents like the NCRI.

The cycle repeated throughout the 2000s. Under the guise of diplomacy with the EU-3 (Britain, France and Germany), Tehran expanded enrichment capacity, refined centrifuge technology, and built a clandestine procurement network. In 2009, it agreed to a Brazilian-Turkish swap deal involving low-enriched uranium. Yet Iran failed to honour the terms. Instead, it accelerated its activities.

Then came the 2015 Joint Comprehensive Plan of Action (JCPOA), championed by President Barack Obama. The deal offered sanctions relief in exchange for temporary nuclear curbs. But it was riddled with flaws. Inspections were restricted to civilian sites like Natanz, while military sites, where the real action was happening, remained off-limits. Key facilities remained intact. Centrifuge R&D was permitted. And billions of dollars in frozen assets were released to a regime whose primary exports are war, terrorism, and misery.

Supporters of the JCPOA argued it delayed Iran's nuclear progress by a decade, but these claims ignored the deal's failure to address military sites and its temporary nature, which allowed Iran to resume enrichment unabated by 2019[4].

Iran's compliance with the JCPOA was short-lived. By 2019, it resumed enrichment beyond agreed limits—first to 20%, then to 60%. It installed advanced IR-6 and IR-8 centrifuges, expanding its capacity exponentially. In 2021, the IAEA revealed that Iran had failed to explain uranium traces at undeclared sites. Inspections were obstructed. Cameras removed. Questions ignored. Negotiations on "JCPOA 2.0" became another exercise in Western wishful thinking.

By early 2025, Iran's stockpile of 60% enriched uranium reached 150 kilograms, sufficient for three nuclear warheads with further enrichment, with a breakout time estimated at two weeks, per a 2024 U.S. intelligence assessment[5].

Hassan Rouhani, Iran's former president and lead nuclear negotiator, admitted in his 2011 memoir that Iran had used earlier talks with the West purely to gain time.[110] While European diplomats heralded breakthroughs, Iran quietly built its uranium conversion plant in Isfahan. The Tehran and Paris Agreements were never about compromise. They were tactical manoeuvres, designed to avoid sanctions while strengthening Iran's nuclear infrastructure.

Even today, the West clings to the illusion that the regime can be reasoned with. But history offers no such comfort. Iran has persistently hidden critical sites, obstructed inspections, and violated every agreement it has ever signed. It maintains secret procurement networks, develops missile delivery systems, and supports terror proxies across the Middle East—all while claiming to pursue peaceful nuclear energy.

Breakout and Backfire: Iran's Nuclear Endgame

In early 2025, Iran's state-run Press TV launched a campaign hailing 83% uranium enrichment as a "triumph of sovereignty," rallying youth support amid economic protests[6]. A country sitting on some of the world's largest reserves of oil and gas does not need nuclear power. What it seeks is nuclear leverage, and the immunity that comes with it.

---

[110] Hannah, John, and Saeed Ghasseminejad. "Rouhani, the Deceiver." Foreign Policy, 21 March 2017. Available at: https://foreignpolicy.com/2017/03/21/rouhani-the-deceiver-iran-nuclear-terrorism-trump-obama/

Domestically, the regime promotes its nuclear program as a symbol of national pride and resistance against Western imperialism, a narrative amplified through state media to rally public support despite economic hardship[7].

The IRGC's shadow looms large. This military-industrial behemoth, answerable only to the Supreme Leader, controls the nuclear apparatus, the missile programme, and the foreign terror network. It operates covert research bodies such as SPND and the METFAZ testing site, which have long escaped meaningful scrutiny. While Western officials speak of "reformists" and "hardliners," the real power rests with the Supreme Leader and his praetorian guard. And their intentions are anything but peaceful.

In parallel with its nuclear ambitions, Tehran has expanded a web of proxy militias across the region that serve as both instruments of destabilisation and shields for its nuclear infrastructure. Groups such as Hezbollah in Lebanon, the Houthis in Yemen, and various militias in Iraq and Syria have been armed, trained, and funded by Iran's Islamic Revolutionary Guard Corps (IRGC). These proxies not only carry out Tehran's foreign policy through asymmetric warfare but also create zones of conflict where international monitoring becomes nearly impossible. In areas controlled by these groups, Iran has greater freedom to transport missile components, test drone technologies, and hide nuclear-linked assets beyond the reach of international inspectors.

In Houthi-controlled Yemen and militia-dominated regions of Iraq, such as Anbar, Iran conceals nuclear-related equipment in underground bunkers, exploiting conflict zones to evade satellite surveillance and IAEA inspections. In February 2025, U.S. naval forces intercepted a Houthi vessel in the Arabian Sea carrying centrifuge components destined for Iran's covert facilities.

More worrying still is the prospect of nuclear cooperation between Iran and other rogue states. Western and Israeli intelligence sources have raised repeated concerns over covert technical exchanges between Iran and North Korea, particularly in the fields of missile delivery systems and centrifuge design. By April 2025, North Korea had shared preliminary nuclear warhead miniaturization designs with Iran, in exchange for ballistic missile technology.

Recent reports also suggest that as Russia's war in Ukraine deepens its isolation from the West, Moscow may be looking to strengthen its strategic ties with Tehran, including support for nuclear development in exchange for drones and weapons.

In 2024, North Korea provided Iran with advanced centrifuge blueprints, while Russia supplied missile guidance systems in exchange for Iranian Shahed drones, per a UN Panel of Experts report.

The late Senator John McCain once said, "The only thing worse than bombing Iran is letting Iran get the bomb." His warning rings truer than ever. Tehran is now closer to nuclear breakout than at any point in its history. Rafael Grossi, speaking at the 2025 World Economic Forum, noted that Iran is "pressing the gas pedal" on enrichment.

In March 2025, the IAEA reported that Iran had further restricted inspector access, with undeclared sites in Fordow showing traces of enriched uranium at 83% purity, perilously close to weapons-grade. Tehran's deployment of additional IR-9 centrifuges, capable of enriching uranium ten times faster than earlier models, signalled an aggressive push toward breakout capacity, underscoring the regime's defiance of international oversight.

Tehran's decades-long pattern of deceit demonstrates that negotiations based on mutual trust are illusory. Any new agreement that does not involve unconditional dismantling of enrichment sites, and complete transparency will simply be another pause in the regime's steady march towards nuclear armament. The lessons of the JCPOA's failure must be heeded: appeasement enables Tehran's ambitions; only credible pressure can halt them.

The path forward is not more concessions, but firm action. The Iranian nuclear dossier must be referred back to the UN Security Council. Sanctions must be reinstated and rigorously enforced. A March 2025 UN Security Council resolution to censure Iran's nuclear violations was vetoed by Russia and China, highlighting the need for unilateral Western measures.

The West must finally shed its illusions. The correct policy is not one of compromise, appeasement, or another flawed deal reminiscent of Barack Obama's JCPOA. Donald Trump must not repeat the same mistake. Offering the regime a path to sanctions relief in exchange for more empty promises would only embolden it further. The only effective strategy is a firm and unyielding position: the regime must be forced to destroy all its ambitious nuclear projects and halt its support for proxy groups that spread terror across the region. Anything less would allow this theocratic dictatorship to continue playing the West, threatening global peace while inching ever closer to the bomb.

13

"First they ignore you, then they laugh at you, then they fight you, then you win."
- Mahatma Gandhi

IRAN'S TRUE RESISTANCE: BUSTING OPPOSITION MYTHS

In discussions about Iran's political future, regime-aligned analysts and some Western policymakers often repeat a dangerously misleading narrative: that the Iranian opposition is hopelessly fragmented, weak, and incapable of leading real change. This narrative, tirelessly pushed by Tehran's lobbyists and echoed in foreign media, serves a clear purpose. It creates the illusion that there is no viable alternative to the ruling theocracy, thus justifying the West's ongoing policy of appeasement and inaction. However, a closer look at the actual dynamics inside Iran and among the Iranian diaspora reveals a very different picture, one of profound polarization between genuine resistance forces and a collection of ineffective, regime-aligned, or opportunistic exile groups.

In reality, the so-called "divisions" within the opposition are largely artificial. The Iranian political landscape today is not a complex mosaic of factions equally vying for leadership. Rather, it is a battlefield between a singular, organized, and deeply rooted opposition coalition formed in 1981 - the National Council of Resistance of Iran (NCRI) and its core organization, the People's Mojahedin Organization of Iran (PMOI/MEK), founded in 1965 - and a handful of scattered exile groups, nostalgic monarchists, and regime insiders posing as reformers who lack any serious base inside Iran.

Busting Myths: False Factions vs. Real Resistance

Many groups claim to be Iran's "opposition," but most operate comfortably in exile, far from the realities of Iran's brutal repression. Their activities, often limited to sporadic media appearances, conferences in luxury hotels, or social media campaigns, create an image of activism but fail to pose any threat to the regime's survival.

Take the far-left ideological groups. Their ideas and 20th-century slogans feel irrelevant to Iran's current challenges. Confined to academic circles abroad, they have virtually no backing inside the country.

Then there are the so-called "reformists," political figures who were once senior members of the Islamic

Republic and who now market themselves as moderates seeking to reform the system from within. Their vision is not regime change but continuity of the regime under a reformist guise. These individuals, having benefited economically and politically under the current regime, advocate for gradual, cosmetic changes that ultimately reinforce the theocracy's longevity. Far from offering a credible alternative, they serve as a safety valve for the regime during times of crisis.

Among the most visible exile groups are the monarchists, centred mainly around Reza Pahlavi, the son of the deposed Shah. Despite their financial resources and media access, these groups suffer from a fundamental disconnect with Iran's realities. The 1979 revolution decisively rejected monarchy. The abuses, corruption, and repression of the Shah's regime are still fresh in the national memory, making the idea of restoring the monarchy an anachronism rather than a serious political proposition. Moreover, the monarchists' tendency to glorify authoritarian rule and the cult-like adulation of the Pahlavi family alienate the vast majority of Iranians, who seek a modern, democratic republic, not a return to dynasty rule.

Not only are these groups disconnected from the grassroots realities inside Iran, but their activities have also at times actively harmed the broader opposition movement. In the aftermath of the 2022 nationwide protests, for instance, Reza Pahlavi's sudden push for political relevance divided opposition ranks, sowing confusion at a critical moment when unity was essential. This fragmentation allowed the regime to regain the initiative and suppress the uprising more effectively. Far from representing a path forward, these exile groups have often inadvertently furthered the regime's divide-and-conquer strategy to dilute and disorient the real forces of change.

The Iranian regime, aware of the real threat posed by organized resistance, has invested heavily in manufacturing a narrative of opposition division. By promoting misleading comparisons between the NCRI/PMOI and these weak factions, Tehran seeks to undermine the legitimacy of the established resistance and confuse international observers.

This strategy is abetted by foreign media outlets that, wittingly or not, serve the regime's disinformation goals. Persian-language channels systematically underreport or distort the activities of the NCRI and PMOI, while amplifying the voices of monarchists, reformists, or recently emerged activists lacking demonstrable support. The blackout on NCRI and PMOI activities is not accidental; it is the result of a concerted political strategy aimed at sidelining the only opposition force with an actual base of support inside Iran.

The consequence of this media bias is a distorted public perception, particularly among audiences outside Iran, who are led to believe that the Iranian opposition is amorphous, leaderless, and hopelessly divided. Inside Iran, however, the situation is very different. Those risking their lives against the regime are acutely aware of which organizations offer a viable path to regime change.

The Unique Role of the NCRI and PMOI: Resistance, Not Exile Activism

In contrast to the fragmented and externally based exile movements, the NCRI and its principal member, the PMOI, represent a disciplined and resilient resistance with operational depth inside Iran.

The PMOI's Resistance Units, the clandestine cells that operate in all major and medium-sized cities of Iran, engage in daily acts of defiance against the regime. These units organize protests, disseminate anti-regime literature, sabotage regime propaganda efforts, and keep the spirit of resistance alive at immense personal risk. Unlike the exile groups whose activism is largely rhetorical, the PMOI's actions inside Iran are tangible, continuous, and strategically coordinated.

Internationally, the NCRI acts as the political voice of the internal resistance. It maintains a permanent representative office in multiple capitals, engages lawmakers and human rights organizations worldwide, and has articulated a detailed plan for Iran's democratic transition, encapsulated in Maryam Rajavi's Ten-Point Plan.[111] This plan—calling for universal suffrage, gender equality, separation of religion and state, and a non-nuclear Iran, has been endorsed by thousands of legislators across Europe and North America.

Maryam Rajavi with Mr Stephen Harper, former Canadian Prime Minister, Mike Pompeo, former US Secretary of State, Mike Pence, former US Vice President, at the Free Iran Summit, Paris, 2024. (Photo: NCRI)

---

[111] "Maryam Rajavi's Ten-point Plan for the Future of Iran." Maryam Rajavi, December 2006. Available at: https://www.maryam-rajavi.com/en/viewpoints/plan-for-future-of-iran/

The regime's own behaviour confirms the seriousness of the NCRI and PMOI threat. Tehran's intelligence services closely monitor and target PMOI activities, launching assassination attempts against its leaders, including the 2018 foiled bombing plot targeting an NCRI rally in Paris.[112] When engaging in hostage negotiations with Western governments, the regime often demands constraints on the NCRI's activities, a clear acknowledgment of its perceived threat.

In fact, the clearest proof of the PMOI's unique status is the regime's singular focus on them. The mullahs take no other group seriously. Scattered monarchists, leftist theorists, or self-styled reformists are not seen as credible threats. Only the PMOI and NCRI are regarded with genuine fear, because they alone have the organizational capacity and ideological clarity to overthrow the regime.

This is why the PMOI has always been the main target of Tehran's machinery of repression. Tens of thousands of PMOI members and supporters were executed during the 1980s, culminating in the horrific 1988 massacre of political prisoners, in which over 30,000 were executed, 90 percent of them PMOI

---

[112] Biesemans, Bart. "In European First, Iranian Envoy Faces Trial over Foiled Bomb Plot." Reuters, 27 November 2020. Available at: https://www.reuters.com/article/world/in-european-first-iranian-envoy-faces-trial-over-foiled-bomb-plot-idUSKBN2870CA/

activists.[113] No other opposition group has been subjected to such a sustained campaign of extermination.

Beyond repression at home, the regime also waged an international campaign of demonization against the PMOI. As part of its appeasement strategy, the West capitulated to Tehran's demands by designating the PMOI as a "terrorist organization", despite contested allegations.[114] This politically motivated blacklisting was not driven by legal standards, but by political expediency aimed at placating the Iranian regime.[115]

Nevertheless, the PMOI refused to surrender. Through years of tireless campaigning and legal battles, they successfully reversed the designation.

---

[113] "Blood-Soaked Secrets: Why Iran's 1988 Prison Massacres Are Ongoing Crimes Against Humanity." Amnesty International, October 2018. Available at: https://www.amnesty.org/en/latest/campaigns/2018/10/blood-soaked-secrets/. "1988 Massacre of Political Prisoners in Iran." National Council of Resistance of Iran, 4 April 2025. Available at: https://www.ncr-iran.org/en/1988-massacre-of-political-prisoners-in-iran/

[114] Norman Kempster, "U.S. Designates 30 Groups as Terrorists," Los Angeles Times, 9 October 1997.

[115] According to The Wall Street Journal, "In 1997, the State Department added the MEK to a list of global terrorist organizations as 'a signal' of the U.S.'s desire for rapprochement with Tehran's reformists, says Martin Indyk, who at the time was assistant secretary of state for Near East Affairs. President Khatami's government 'considered it a pretty big deal,' Mr. Indyk says." Andrew Higgins and Jay Solomon, "Strange Bedfellows- Iranian Imbroglio Gives New Boost To Odd Exile Group," The Wall Street Journal, 29 November 2006. Available at: https://www.wsj.com/articles/SB116475111368234891

They won every major court case, first in the UK in 2008 and then in the EU in 2009, and the EU officially removed the PMOI from its blacklist. In 2012, the U.S. State Department did the same, removing the PMOI from the list following a court order.

While these victories restored the PMOI's legal status, the damage inflicted by the blacklisting years was substantial. By isolating and stigmatizing the PMOI at a critical historical moment, Western governments inadvertently helped the regime survive. The blacklisting demoralized segments of the opposition, distorted international understanding, and deprived the Iranian people of vital international solidarity when they needed it most. The financial and human resources and attention of the PMOI were also consumed by efforts to secure delisting over a 15-year period.

No other group endures such sustained hostility from the regime, fields an operational network inside Iran, or offers a viable political vision for the country's future.

This singularity sets the NCRI and PMOI apart from the rhetoric and symbolic activism of the broader exile community. Their endurance is not just a matter of survival; it is a living testament to their capacity to lead. Despite assassination attempts, despite political blacklisting, despite systematic censorship in foreign Persian-language media, the PMOI has continued to build Resistance Units inside Iran and to carry out organized acts of civil defiance against overwhelming odds.

This resistance draws on a legacy begun in 1965 with the PMOI's founding. On 6 September 1965, three young Muslim intellectuals, Mohammad Hanifnejad, Saeid Mohsen, and Ali Asghar Badizadegan, founded a clandestine study group that later morphed into the People's Mojahedin Organisation of Iran (PMOI or MEK), the principal and longest-standing Iranian opposition movement. From its very inception, the PMOI rejected both monarchy and religious dictatorship, offering instead a vision of democratic, progressive, and secular governance for Iran.

From 1965 to 1969, the founders were focused on recruiting new members and creating a network of elite cadres that could lead the movement through the anticipated political repression. The first people to join the movement were young intellectuals and university students. Among them was Massoud Rajavi, a young law student who would later play a pivotal role in reviving the organization and shaping its future.[116]

During the winter of 1969, the PMOI began to form a network of activists that could start taking concrete

---

[116] "Massoud Rajavi, Founder of the NCRI," National Council of Resistance of Iran, accessed April 2025. Available at: https://www.ncr-iran.org/en/massoud-rajavi/

action against the Shah's regime. In August 1971, while the Iranian monarchy was preparing for its lavish celebrations of its lengthy rule, the Shah ordered a widespread crackdown on all opposition groups and individuals that could prove problematic to the ceremonies. In a sweeping raid against the PMOI, SAVAK arrested and incarcerated more than 90 percent of its members, including all of its leaders.

The stories of the PMOI's resistance in the Shah's prisons and courts circulated among Iranians by word of mouth, and soon the organization built a solid and widespread base of support in Iranian society. On 25 May 1972, the Shah's regime executed Mohammad Hanifnejad, Saeid Mohsen, and Ali Asghar Badizadegan.

Of all the leading members of the PMOI, only Massoud Rajavi was saved from imminent death thanks to an international campaign led by his elder brother, Dr. Kazem Rajavi.[117] Kazem, a renowned jurist and academic in Switzerland, rallied several organizations and politicians to intervene and pressure the Shah to revoke Massoud's death sentence. Among those politicians was François Mitterrand, leader of the French Socialist Party, who later became President of France. Under intense

---

[117] "Prof. Kazem Rajavi, Iran's great defender of human rights," PMOI website, 29 August 2020. Available at:
https://english.mojahedin.org/article/prof-kazem-rajavi-irans-great-defender-of-human-rights/

international pressure, the Shah was forced to commute Massoud's death sentence to life imprisonment.

Prof. Kazem Rajavi (Photo: NCRI)

In late 1973, a group of self-styled Marxists took advantage of the absence of the PMOI's original leadership and carried out a bloody coup within the organization. They declared that it had become Marxist.[118] They went as far as intimidating and oppressing PMOI members who remained loyal to the organization's true principles, murdering opponents

---

[118] U.S. State Department, unclassified background report on the MEK, December 1984.

like Majid Sharif-Vaghefi and purging half the rank-and-file. The turmoil almost tore the PMOI apart.

Yet, even from behind prison walls, Massoud Rajavi rejected the coup and worked to rebuild the PMOI. His efforts ensured that the core ideals of the movement, democracy, independence, and secularism, would endure.

On 20 January 1979, merely 10 days before Khomeini returned to Iran, Massoud Rajavi and other leading members of the PMOI were released from the Shah's prisons.

A Proper Future: Iran's Democratic Hope

The overthrow of the Shah marked not only the end of a dynastic monarchy steeped in repression and excess but also the beginning of a darker era that betrayed the hopes of the revolution. What began as a nationwide outcry for liberty, justice, and dignity was soon hijacked by religious fundamentalism, plunging Iran into a theocratic dictatorship far more brutal than the regime it replaced.

While the Shah's authoritarianism drove many Iranians to despair, the subsequent rise of Khomeini's regime extinguished any remaining hopes for pluralism and freedom. Yet from the ashes of monarchy and the betrayal of revolution, a new resistance emerged. Embodied by the founders of the

PMOI and continued by its committed members, this movement has offered a vision of Iran that transcends both crown and turban, a democratic republic rooted in tolerance, justice, and the genuine aspirations of the Iranian people.

The story of Iran's modern history is not one of helpless victimhood, but of unyielding resistance, and the first chapter of that story has only just begun.

14

"If you tell a lie big enough and keep repeating it, people will eventually come to believe it."
- Joseph Goebbels

THE IRANIAN REGIME'S MISINFORMATION CAMPAIGN

Propaganda and misinformation have long been used as aggressive weapons, exploited to undermine the morale of the enemy and to wear down the will of an opponent to fight. By manipulating the news, successes on the side of the propagandist can be exaggerated or even invented. The moral superiority of the cause against which the opponent is fighting can be falsified and lies and demonization of the opponent's leaders can be spread to disintegrate resistance by fabricating evidence that the people who support the opponent have been deceived and misled. Throughout history, such tactics have been commonplace, with the Nazis even appointing Joseph Goebbels as their Second World War Propaganda Minister.

The Iranian regime has borrowed heavily from the Nazi playbook, using propaganda and the tactics of demonization to traduce the PMOI, whom it regards as an arch enemy, and to confuse the public at home and abroad.

Weaponizing Lies: Iran's Anti-PMOI Propaganda Machine

The Iranian regime employs an extensive arsenal of communication tools - state media, films, television programmes, book publishing, social media - for the dissemination of false information, and to instil fear, doubt, and distrust among the public, particularly the youth. It aims to tarnish the image of the PMOI and propagate the notion that no credible democratic alternative exists, thereby justifying continued Western appeasement toward the regime.

IRGC and MOIS operatives leverage platforms like Telegram and X, deploying thousands of fake accounts and bot networks to amplify anti-PMOI narratives and sow distrust among Iranian youth, as documented by the Centre for Countering Digital Hate, a British-American not-for-profit NGO, with offices in London and Washington D.C. (CCDH, 2024).

The regime's reliance on propaganda has surged markedly since 2017, a year that witnessed the eruption of widespread protests across Iran, signalling the depth of public discontent. In the wake of these protests, and further exacerbated by the nationwide demonstrations of 2019, the state's media apparatus intensified its campaign of vilification against the PMOI, which senior officials believe organized the protests.[119] Between 2017 and 2019 alone, state-controlled television networks aired no fewer than ten propaganda documentaries and a sprawling multi-part series designed to demonize the opposition movement.

One particularly noteworthy example was the documentary titled *Sarcheshmeh* ("The Origin"),[120] whose first season comprised 20 episodes, each

---

[119] In a speech delivered shortly after the outbreak of major protests in December 2017, Supreme Leader Ali Khamenei openly acknowledged the pivotal role of the PMOIPMOI. Drawing upon what he described as evidence and intelligence, Khamenei remarked, "The PMOIPMOI had prepared for this [protest] months ago... The PMOIPMOI's media outlet had called for it" (Khamenei's official website, 9 January 2018. Available at: http://english.khamenei.ir/news/5394/Recent-damage-inflicted-on-Iran-by-U-S-will-gain-a-response. Similarly, in a televised address in January 2020, Khamenei decried Albania, headquarters of the PMOI, as a "small and sinister" nation, accusing it of harbouring thousands of "treacherous" members of the PMOI. He further alleged that the PMOI had orchestrated the nationwide protests of November 2019. Khamenei's remarks provoked swift rebuttals from Albanian officials, who dismissed his accusations as baseless and inflammatory. For further details, see "Albanian Leaders Dismiss Khamenei's Purported 'Sinister' Smear," Radio Free Europe/Radio Liberty, 9 January 2020. Available at: https://www.rferl.org/a/albanian-leaders-dismiss-khamenei-s-purported-sinister-smear/30368335.html
[120] See "We are explicit in Sarcheshmeh," Quds Online, 25 December 2019.

lasting approximately 50 minutes. This single production alone represents over 1,000 minutes of calculated disinformation.

Such an extensive investment of airtime underscores the regime's desperate attempt to rewrite the narrative and suppress the growing resonance of the PMOI's message among an increasingly restive populace.
Amidst further crises, particularly following the 2022 uprising and the regime's entanglement in a regional conflict of its own making, the threat posed by the PMOI to the regime has significantly intensified, as has the regime's desperate attempts to undermine their image. Until 2020, the regime published over 500 books against the PMOI, averaging 12–13 books annually, according to opposition estimates.[121] In other words, over the course of 41 years, the regime has published an average of 13 books annually against the PMOI.

Iran's Ministry of Intelligence and Security (MOIS) and the IRGC proliferate distorted facts and numerous slurs against the PMOI, claims that lawmakers, senior researchers, universities, scholars, and reputable think tanks in the United States and

---

[121] "Iran Regime Publishes Books in a Desperate Attempt to Demonize the PMOI," National Council of Resistance of Iran, 5 October 2020. Available at: https://www.ncr-iran.org/en/news/iran-resistance/iran-regime-publishes-books-in-a-desperate-attempt-to-demonize-the-PMOI/

Europe have, over many years, debunked repeatedly.[122] Iran, under its so-called 'moderate' president Masoud Pezeshkian, a puppet of the increasingly paranoid Ali Khamenei, continues to be globally recognised as a leading executioner and state sponsor of terrorism and warmongering.

In March 2025, MOIS cyber operatives launched a global disinformation campaign on Instagram, using 5,000 fake accounts to spread fabricated PMOI terror allegations, targeting Iranian diaspora communities, per the Cyber Threat Alliance (CTA Report, 2025). It is therefore essential to examine, one by one, its main lines of denunciation of the PMOI, to understand the truth.

The PMOI and the National Council of Resistance of Iran (NCRI)

Its appeal among youth and women, fuelled by decades of regime repression, stems from organized

---

[122] For example, in July 2019, a prominent bipartisan American delegation visited thousands of PMOI activists in Albania. According to their subsequent report, they observed a highly organized and cohesive political movement led by a dynamic and capable female leadership. The movement, they said, is characterized by a clearly articulated political platform and supported by an extensive network of dedicated supporters both within Iran and across the globe, all committed to realizing its vision for a democratic future. (Sheehan, Ivan Sascha. Iran's Resurgent Resistance: Bipartisan U.S. Delegation Visits with PMOI Opposition at Ashraf 3. Iran Policy Committee, 2020). Available at: https://www.amazon.com/Irans-Resurgent-Resistance-Bipartisan-Delegation/dp/1734229209

resistance units and a clear 10-point democratic plan, making it a prime target for Tehran's propaganda, as noted by the Atlantic Council (2024).

The PMOI is often described by the MOIS and IRGC in interviews to targeted Western media, as "Islamic Marxists," a label crafted by the Shah's notorious secret police (SAVAK) and later expanded by the mullahs' regime.[123] In a revealing interview on 26 November 2023, with Manoto TV, a Persian TV channel, Parviz Sabeti, the former head of SAVAK's third directorate, and a key figure in overseeing torture and executions of dissidents in the Shah's prisons, clarified the origins of this characterisation. Sabeti stated, "From the very first report I submitted to His Majesty (The Shah), I said that they were an Islamic group, and that they later adopted Marxism,

---

[123] Iranian scholar Afshin Matin-Asgari characterizes the term "Islamic Marxism" as an "ingenious polemical label" crafted by the Shah's regime during the 1970s. This term was deliberately employed to discredit and delegitimize its most formidable adversaries, encapsulating the regime's strategy of rhetorical vilification to undermine opposition movements. (Matin-Asgari, Afshin. 2004. *From social democracy to social democracy: the twentieth-century odyssey of the Iranian Left*. In: Cronin, Stephanie, editor. *Reformers and Revolutionaries in Modern Iran: New Perspectives on the Iranian Left*: London and New York: RoutledgeCurzon. p 37-64). Available at: https://www.routledge.com/Reformers-and-Revolutionaries-in-Modern-Iran-New-Perspectives-on-the-Iranian-Left/Cronin/p/book/9780415573443?srsltid=AfmBOooHnQh6nPTUoRthvcuC3L76B5tVbc-4F7fz1CypUNfzu2fSi4n5

and thus the label of 'Islamic Marxist' was affixed to them."[124]

In an interview with Time magazine on 14 September 1981, Massoud Rajavi, the leader of the Iranian Resistance, said, "Every high school student knows that believing in God, Jesus Christ and Muhammad is incompatible with the philosophy of Marxism. Everyone knows that, even Khomeini. But for dictators like Khomeini, "Marxist Islamic" is a very profitable phrase to use against any opposition. If Jesus Christ and Muhammad were alive and protesting against Khomeini, he would call them Marxists, too."[125]

Many experts, even those not favourably inclined towards the PMOI, have highlighted this point. Syracuse University professor Mehrzad Boroujerdi wrote: "Rajavi saves his most extensive critical commentary for Marxist materialistic epistemology.... The group remained sceptical of Marxism's philosophical postulates and rejected the latter's cardinal doctrine of historical materialism. It held firm to the beliefs in the existence of God, revelation, the afterlife, the spirit, salvation, destiny, and the

---

[124] Interview with Manoto TV Channel, November 23, 2023. On YouTube (in Farsi). Available at:
https://www.youtube.com/watch?v=EpK7ircr6Tk
[125] "We are on the Offensive," Time, 14 September 1981. Available at: https://time.com/archive/6858729/we-are-on-the-offensive/

people's commitment to these intangible principles."[126]

The Iranian regime also promotes assertions that the PMOI is a terrorist organisation. In fact, the PMOI was removed from all terrorist lists as a result of multiple high-profile judicial rulings in their favour. Competent courts in the United Kingdom, the European Union, and the United States unanimously ordered the relevant ministries to remove the terrorist designation and strongly criticised the prolongation of such politically motivated designations.

In the summer of 2024, the Iranian regime's notorious judiciary announced the start of trials in absentia of the PMOI and 104 members of the Resistance, including many of its leaders and many who have been refugees in Ashraf 3, Albania, or in France and other countries for decades. During this sham trial, many of the regime's officials who support these sham trials aim to thwart the PMOI's influence, especially among the younger generation, and to initiate legal proceedings against the PMOI abroad and pave the way for the imposition of pressure and restrictions against them abroad, including through Interpol Red Notices.

---

[126] Boroujerdi, Mehrzad, *Iranian Intellectuals and the West: The Tormented Triumph of Nativism* (Syracuse: Syracuse University Press, 1996), pp. 117-119. Available at:
https://www.amazon.com/Iranian-Intellectuals-West-Tormented-Intellectual/dp/0815604335

However, past experiences reveal that beyond these stated goals, the regime harbours a more sinister objective, namely, laying the groundwork for terrorist activities against the PMOI in Europe. Particularly egregious is the framing of the PMOI in this bogus trial in absentia for crimes such as "waging war against God" and "corruption on earth," offenses punishable by death.

In 2025, the regime intensified its propaganda offensive. State television launched a new 15-episode series called "The Shadow of Betrayal," in which it admitted that the PMOI had organized the 2022-2023 uprisings, which aired in January 2025 on 600 minutes. (IRIB Schedule, 2025).

Global Infiltration and the Call to Confront Propaganda

Iranian regime intelligence officials have publicly admitted that they use "friendly journalists" to promote Tehran's anti-PMOI narrative in the West. Perhaps most notably, a former Minister of Intelligence, Ali Fallahian, who is sought by German and Swiss judiciaries for terrorism, said on 9 July 2017: "The Intelligence Ministry needs a cover to gather intelligence, whether inside or outside (Iran). We don't send an intelligence agent to Germany or America who says, 'I am from the Ministry of

Intelligence.' Rather, an entrepreneurial or journalistic cover is required for this."[127]

Some Western journalists and academics have exposed the regime's campaign. Shane Harris, at the time an investigative reporter with the Daily Beast, has written that, "An Iranian activist group, backed by the country's intelligence service, is trying to enlist American journalists and academics in a propaganda campaign. ... I speak from experience because the group recently tried to recruit me."[128] Similarly, the Canadian newspaper Toronto Sun revealed that John Thompson of the Mackenzie Institute think tank "was offered $80,000 by a man tied to Iran's mission in Canada. He said: "They wanted me to publish a piece on the Mujahedin-e Khalq. ... Iran is trying to get other countries to label it as a terrorist cult." Thompson says he turned down the offer."[129]

In 2022, Albania's media, citing the country's Intelligence sources, revealed that in addition to cyberattacks against Tirana, the Iranian regime's "extra-territorial intelligence unit of the IRGC's Quds

---

[127] Iran: Using "Journalist" Cover by Mullahs' Ministry of Intelligence, NCRI Foreign Affairs Committee, 24 May 2019. Ali Fallahian, interview, Aparat TV, 9 July 2017. Available at: https://twitter.com/Ashrafi4ever/status/1097574573195911168

[128] Shane Harris, "Iran's Spies Tried to Recruit Me," The Daily Beast, 14 June 2015. Available at:
https://www.thedailybeast.com/irans-spies-tried-to-recruit-me/

[129] Toronto Sun, 5 July 2020. Available at:
http://web.archive.org/web/20100708150317/https://torontosun.com/news/canada/2010/07/05/14616126.html

Force secret operations also dispatched secret agents to vilify PMOI members. To this end, this unit also attempted to infiltrate the Albanian media."[130]

The regime's propaganda has penetrated other European media. In Germany, for example, Der Spiegel has published cruel stories of the PMOI torturing its members in Ashraf 3 and practicing how to kill people without weapons. But almost immediately, German courts ordered the weekly to remove the ridiculous charges against the PMOI. According to the Associated Press on 26 March 2019, the court ordered Der Spiegel to remove from its article the paragraphs alleging that an Iranian opposition group was involved in "torture" and "creating psychological fear" because they did not correspond to reality. According to the report, the Hamburg court threatened to pay a fine of €250,000 if the magazine did not remove these points about the PMOI headquarters in Albania. The ruling comes at a difficult time for Der Spiegel, as it was revealed in December that a prominent award-winning journalist for the magazine had been sacked for inventing quotes and details in some of his own articles. Having no evidence to support its accusations against the PMOI, Der Spiegel complied.

---

[130] "Iran Trying to Spread Fake News via Albanian Journalists," Albania Daily News, 19 December 2022. Available at: https://albaniandailynews.com/news/iran-trying-to-spread-fake-news-via-albanian-journalists

In the UK, both Channel 4 News and the Guardian have run smear stories targeting the Iranian refugees in Albania, likening them to a cult and claiming they live in a tightly secured military compound. One absurd article even alleged the PMOI had kidnapped and murdered some of their own supporters. The claims were preposterous and easily disproved.[131] Indeed, three weeks before the reports appeared on Channel 4 News and in the Guardian, the same reports were published almost word for word in a website created by Massoud Khodabandeh and Anne Singleton, two notorious MOIS agents.[132] This

---

[131] "Letters to the Guardian, Warning Against Iran Regime's Plans to Exploit the Newspaper and Set the Stage for Terrorism Against the Opposition," NCRI, 1 November 2018. Available at: https://www.ncr-iran.org/en/news/iran-resistance/letters-to-the-guardian-warning-against-iran-regime-s-plans-to-exploit-the-newspaper-and-set-the-stage-for-terrorism-against-the-opposition/

[132] A December 2012 investigative report by the Pentagon unveiled that Anne Singleton and Massoud Khodabandeh are operatives of Iran's Ministry of Intelligence and Security (MOIS). The report further highlighted that the website *Interlink.org* was established explicitly at the behest of the Tehran regime, serving as a propaganda tool aligned with MOIS directives. The 64-page document, titled *"Iran's Ministry of Intelligence and Security: A Profile,"* was produced under an Interagency Agreement with the Combating Terrorism Technical Support Office's Irregular Warfare Support Program. Released by the Federal Research Division of the Library of Congress, the report provides a comprehensive examination of MOIS activities, shedding light on its methods of disinformation and infiltration to undermine opposition movements abroad. See "Iran's Ministry of Intelligence and Security: A Profile," The Library of Congress, December 2012. Available at: https://archive.org/details/IransMinistryOfIntelligenceAndSecurityAProfile

exposed the sinister source of the prejudicial fake news. Soon after these articles appeared the Albanians uncovered further plots by the Iranian ambassador and his gang to organize bomb plots,[133] assassinations and cyberattacks, the Iranian embassy was finally closed, and the ambassador and his diplomats expelled.[134]

The demonization machinery is still at work and aids and abets the Western policy of appeasement. The regime has infiltrated its agents into the very heart of our western democracies. In the European Parliament until recently, every time a motion was tabled criticizing the mullahs, the senior advisor to the Socialist group on Middle Eastern affairs, Eldar Mamedov, a Latvian with Iranian origins, always briefed against the authors of the motion and put down pro-regime amendments. It was always assumed Mamedov was controlled by the mullahs. When the Qatargate corruption scandal erupted in the European Parliament, Mamedov was quickly exposed

---

[133] "Albania says it foiled Iranian plot to attack exiled dissidents," Reuters, 23 October 2019. Available at:
https://www.reuters.com/article/world/albania-says-it-foiled-iranian-plot-to-attack-exiled-dissidents-idUSKBN1X22CM/
[134] Fatos Bytyci and Florion Goga, "Albanian police search empty Iranian embassy after papers burned," Reuters, 8 September 2022. Available at: https://www.reuters.com/world/middle-east/iranian-diplomats-burn-documents-hours-before-leaving-albania-2022-09-08/

as one of the key officials involved.[135] He was immediately dismissed from the Socialist group.

Individual MEPs in the European Parliament and MPs in Western democracies are often singled out for an onslaught of misinformation, whenever they express support for the PMOI or call for freedom and democracy in Iran. They are often bombarded with misinformation about the PMOI and can often also receive calls from the Iranian embassy or from people who claim to be disaffected former members of the PMOI, although they are in fact trained MOIS agents who have been recruited by the regime.

In September 2023, the London-based TV station 'Iran International' and the news website 'Semafor' sent shockwaves through Europe and America when they revealed that an influential organization known as the Iran Experts Initiative (IEI), which had consistently lobbied and advised the Biden administration, EU governments and the European Parliament, was in fact set up and controlled by Tehran, stirring profound implications for global diplomacy and security. Based on an avalanche of leaked emails translated from Farsi into English by Iran International and Semafor, the two news organizations showed how the so-called 'Experts

---

[135] "S&D adviser Eldar Mamedov suspended amid EU Qatar probe," POLITICO, 22 December 2022. Available at: https://www.politico.eu/article/sd-adviser-eldar-mamedov-suspended-amid-eu-qatar-probe/

Network' had been created by the mullahs' regime in 2014 "to improve Tehran's image abroad".[136] Experts from the network had consistently peddled misleading information designed by the mullahs, while also demonizing the NCRI and the PMOI.[137]

The leaked emails exposed how the theocratic regime sought to use the Experts Network to build international ties with influential academics and researchers, penetrating governments, think tanks and advisory groups at the highest level and spreading the regime's propaganda in Western media. They revealed the disturbing fact that European governments and institutions were relying on analyses and recommendations for their policy on Iran provided by these so-called experts.[138] The emails unmasked the Iranian regime's covert initiative to

---

[136] Jay Solomon, "Inside Iran's Influence Operation," SEMAFOR, 29 September 2023. Available at:
https://www.semafor.com/article/09/25/2023/inside-irans-influence-operation

[137] For example, one of the "experts," Ariane Tabatabai called the PMOI a "cult" back in 2014 in one of her first published articles. ("Beware of the PMOI," The National Interest, 22 August 2014. Available at: https://nationalinterest.org/feature/beware-the-PMOI-11118

[138] One of the exposed "experts" in the regime's network, Rouzbeh Parsi, the brother of Trita Parsi, the Iranian regime's chief lobbyist and former head of the National Iranian American Council (NIAC) lobbying group in Washington, wrote a policy paper for the European Union Institute for Security Studies, where he said, "It should be stressed here that the PMOI is not a viable and legitimate interlocutor." (Rouzbeh Parsi, "Iran in the shadow of the 2009 presidential elections," European Union Institute for Security Studies, April 2011. Available at: https://ciaotest.cc.columbia.edu/wps/ceps/0022671/f_0022671_18656.pdf

advance Tehran's interests, including its nuclear programme, while diverting attention from its appalling human rights record. One of the members of this network, Arian Tabatabaei, had been appointed advisor to the US Deputy Secretary of Defence for Special Operations, while Adnan Tabatabaei was an advisor to the German Foreign Ministry, and Roozbeh Parsi was an advisor to the Swedish Foreign Ministry.

When Western media outlets play the role of useful idiots for the Iranian regime, it is worth remembering Voltaire's statement: "Those who can make you believe absurdities can make you commit atrocities." Disgracefully, some newspapers and TV channels, like the New York Times, Der Spiegel, Frankfurter Allgemeine, the Guardian and Channel 4 News, have been seduced by the regime's demonization campaign. They are the willing tools of the regime. When this evil dictatorship is toppled, history will record the names of those who played this dishonest game in a roll call of shame.

In a shocking example, the New York Times wrote in a February 16, 2020 article entitled "Highly Secretive Iranian Rebels Barricaded in Albania. They gave us a tour."[139] The main witness to the charges was a person

---

[139] Patrick Kingsley, "Highly Secretive Iranian Rebels Are Holed Up in Albania. They Gave Us a Tour," The New York Times, 16 February 2020. Available at:
https://www.nytimes.com/2020/02/16/world/europe/iran-mek-albania.html

named Abdolrahman Mohammadian, who had left the ranks of the PMOI many years ago and had joined the regime's service and was living in Albania. He had made many accusations against the Mojahedin, but in January 2025, Mohammadian sent a letter to Antonio Guterres, UN Secretary-General, acknowledging that at the time of his interview with the New York Times for this article, he had in fact been recruited by Iran's Ministry of Intelligence and Security (MOIS). He admitted that all the points he and his colleagues had made in that interview were lies and had been dictated directly to them by the Ministry of Intelligence. He wrote, "I hope that by writing this letter, the burden of my sins and mistakes will be reduced to cooperate with this network."[140]

Until that happens, the theocratic regime's mercenaries in Europe who have posed deceptively as refugees, experts, and scholars should have their passports and citizenship revoked. Critics warn that closing Iran's embassies could disrupt diplomatic channels and trade, but such arguments ignore the embassies' role as hubs for terrorism and propaganda, perpetuating a cycle of appeasement. Known agents from the MOIS and Quds Force should be arrested, prosecuted, and expelled. Iran's network of

---

[140] "Enlightening letter of MOIS agent
6 years of cooperation with the Iranian regime's Ministry of Intelligence, MOIS in Albania," Iran Probe, 11 March 2025. Available at: https://iranprobe.com/enlightening-letter-of-mois-agent/

embassies, which they use as bomb factories and terrorist cells, should be closed down and their so-called diplomats banished.

15

> "Power tends to corrupt, and absolute power corrupts absolutely."
> - *Lord Acton*

A PUPPET IN POWER: PEZESHKIAN AND THE SUPREME LEADER'S SCRIPT

In a bid to quell another revolution that could sweep his regime from power, the ageing Supreme Leader Ayatollah Ali Khamenei engineered the sham election of Ebrahim Raisi as president in 2021. As deputy prosecutor in Tehran in 1988, he was one of four individuals whom the then Supreme Leader, Ruhollah Khomeini, appointed to a 'death commission'[141] in Tehran to massacre supporters of the opposition PMOI. It is estimated that thirty thousand political prisoners were summarily executed within a few months.[142]

---

[141] "Iran: President Raisi's death must not deny victims of his grim human rights legacy their right to accountability", Amnesty International, 22 May 2024. Available at:
https://www.amnesty.org/en/latest/news/2024/05/iran-president-raisis-death-must-not-deny-victims-of-his-grim-human-rights-legacy-their-right-to-accountability/
[142] Reza Malek, a former intelligence officer, revealed that according to documents he had personally seen, 33,700

For his zeal as a merciless executioner, Raisi was promoted to Tehran prosecutor. He later became deputy head of the judiciary, then judiciary chief, paving his way to the presidency as the ultimate, bloodstained hardliner. Raisi was placed on the U.S. Treasury blacklist in 2019 for serial human rights violations.[143]

During his tenure as president, more than 2,000 people were executed. Many young protesters were arrested during the nationwide uprising in 2022-23. It was somewhat ironic that Raisi, the "Butcher of Tehran", met his end in an American helicopter. When the U.S.-made Bell 212 helicopter plummeted into a mountainside on 19 May 2024, in Northern Iran, it ended the life of one of the greatest criminals in Iranian and modern world history. For him, it was a fittingly fiery and deserving end to a murderous career.

Raisi's death plunged the Iranian regime into an unprecedented crisis. Ninety million Iranians were sick of the theocratic regime, their corruption and incompetence, and their squandering the nation's wealth on foreign proxy-wars and terrorism, turning Iran into an international pariah. The ruling elite's factional

---

prisoners were executed in 1988. Available at: https://iran1988.org/1988-massacre/
[143] "Treasury Designates Supreme Leader of Iran's Inner Circle Responsible for Advancing Regime's Domestic and Foreign Oppression", U.S. Department of the Treasury, 4 November 2019. Available at: https://home.treasury.gov/news/press-releases/sm824

feuding, as they struggled to cling to power, brought Iran to its knees. The death of Raisi, seen as favourite to succeed the ailing 86-year-old Supreme Leader, so destabilised the regime that Khamenei moved quickly to find a replacement who, under the bogus guise of a moderate, could quell rising dissent among the rebellious youth.

A former heart surgeon, Masoud Pezeshkian, won the second round of the sham presidential elections in Iran in the lowest electoral turnout since 1979.[144] When asked what his policies would be as president, Pezeshkian replied: "Khamenei sets all plans and policies and straying from them is my redline."[145]

---

[144] "Iran announces record low election turnout despite calls on voters to participate", CNN, 4 March 2024. Available at: https://www.cnn.com/2024/03/04/middleeast/iran-low-turnout-election-intl/index.html

[145] State-run news agency ISNA, 19 June 2024. Available at (in Farsi): https://www.isna.ir/news/1403033020817/پزشکیان-هرچه-با-سیاست-های-کلی-رهبری-تطابق-نداشته-باشد-خط-قرمز

Newly inaugurated Iranian regime President Masoud Pezeshkian meets privately with Khamenei shortly after his election, in a meeting arranged to affirm alignment between the presidency and the Supreme Leader following his 5th of July win. (Photo: Office of Iran regime's Supreme Leader)

For decades Western appeasers have grasped at straws trying to convince themselves that the future of Iran could be secured if only a 'reformist' or 'moderate' president could take the helm. This delusional theory ignored the fact that the Supreme Leader has ultimate authority in the Islamic Republic and the role of president is simply that of a puppet or a "tea boy," as former president Mohammad Khatami famously said.[146]

---

[146] Mohammad Mehdi Tehrani, "Revisting a Contradiction: Am I a quartermaster, or Am I not?" Raja News website, 10 March 2009. Available at: https://www.rajanews.com/news/10392

When Hassan Rouhani was president, he was hailed as a reformist, despite the fact that he presided over the continuing sponsorship of Bashar al-Assad in Syria, the Houthi rebels in Yemen, the vicious Shi'ite militias in Iraq, the terrorist Hezbollah in Lebanon, and Hamas in Gaza, as well as the Islamic Revolutionary Guard Corps (IRGC) and their terror tactics through the Middle East and further afield. Rouhani even masterminded the plan to send Assadollah Assadi, a sitting Iranian diplomat in Vienna, to blow up a mass Iranian opposition rally in Paris in 2018 with a professionally constructed 0.5 kg TATP bomb. Rouhani was no moderate, but appeasers in the West fell for the ploy.

The mass boycott of the sham presidential election showed that the people of Iran have said no to the theocratic dictatorship of the mullahs and yes to the overthrow of the regime and its replacement with a democratic, secular republic. The Iranian people have had enough.

The international community must recognize the right of the Iranian people and organized opposition units to use all means at their disposal to resist the ruthless machinery of suppression and to overthrow the mullahs. The so-called 'moderate' and 'reformist' president of Iran, Masoud Pezeshkian, quickly demonstrated his willingness to acquiesce to the policies of the Supreme Leader by launching an ideological purge of teachers and university professors that had echoes of the darkest days of Stalin's Soviet Union.

More than 20,000 school principals were removed from their posts in a punitive shake-up, according to reports in the state-run newspaper Etemad. Apparently, the move was part of a broader strategy to eliminate dissent and enforce loyalty within the country's educational system. The teachers targeted were believed to have been involved in widespread protests that broke out in schools and colleges across Iran during the nationwide uprising in 2022/23. Teachers and students took to the streets in towns and cities across Iran, voicing their dissent with the theocratic regime and calling for the mullahs' overthrow.

The backlash was not limited to school principals. The clerical regime also targeted university professors. 32,000 associate professors were dismissed and replaced by first and second-semester doctoral students, deemed to be loyal propagators of the mullahs' repressive ideology, specially trained for their new roles in hastily convened 40-hour courses. President Pezeshkian was following the example of his hard-line predecessor, Ebrahim Raisi, the 'Butcher of Tehran'. Raisi began a purge of university professors early in his presidency, in a bid to "purify" universities by removing those who failed to show unwavering loyalty to the Supreme Leader Ali Khamenei and the Islamic regime's fundamentalist principles.

Those professional teachers and professors summarily fired from their jobs now face bleak employment prospects in Iran's collapsing economy. Already many have fled abroad, accelerating a brain drain that has caused a sharp deterioration in Iranian education, with inevitable impacts on many sectors. Of course, confronted with news of the educational purge, Iran's Education Minister Reza Morad Sahraee denied it was happening and said the turnover was a routine annual occurrence.

Pezeshkian has been hailed by many western politicians and journalists as a reformist, who could herald a brighter future for Iran's beleaguered 90 million population. He is a wolf in sheep's clothing and has repeatedly confirmed that he will stick rigidly to the policy of the Supreme Leader. Indeed, during his election campaign, he was booed by students after he made flattering comments about Khamenei. He angrily responded by saying: "I accept the leadership; I am completely devoted to him… You have no right to insult someone I believe in. You have no right to disrespect someone I believe in."

The purge of academia in Iran has served to highlight the mullahs' fear that a further nationwide insurrection, fuelled by intellectual independence, could lead to their overthrow. The vast majority who took to the streets in the 2022/23 uprising were rebellious students and young people, often led by women, who hate the misogynist mullahs and deeply object to the repressive female dress codes and mandatory hijab. The protests became much more than a demand for a relaxation of women's dress codes, however, erupting for the first time into furious political demands for regime change.

Primary and secondary school pupils who participated in the walkouts and protests in girls' schools across Iran were subjected to revenge poison gas attacks, leaving many pupils seriously ill. The girls affected reported the smell of tangerine or rotten fish before falling ill. Hundreds were taken to hospital suffering from respiratory problems, nausea, dizziness and fatigue. Several girls died. Gas attacks were reported in Qom, Isfahan, Tabriz, Urmia, Ilam, Shiraz and the capital, Tehran. The mullahs lamely tried to blame foreigners or internal opponents of the regime. Some politicians even accused emotionally charged adolescents of making false claims about the gas attacks. But it is clear that hard-line factions within the IRGC were behind the assaults, which they saw as a way of punishing the schoolgirls for joining the nationwide 'Women, Resistance, Freedom' uprising.

The wave of dismissals underscores the mullahs' desperation to maintain control over the educational sector, although the regime's heavy-handed approach will only serve to deepen discontent and alienate the very individuals tasked with shaping the nation's future. Only a week after Pezeshkian's sham election as president, thousands took to the streets on Sunday 14 July 2024 to protest collapsing welfare conditions and to demand regime change, convinced that the mullahs are incapable of reform.

As prices and inflation skyrocket, the majority of the population now struggles to survive on income that has fallen below the international poverty line. Protesters denounced the incompetence of the government, chanting: "Shout for your rights! We will only obtain our rights in the streets." As the economic crisis deepens, the Iranian regime is facing mounting pressure from its citizens, who are demanding that their basic civil rights and needs be met. The continued protests across the country suggest that the regime's grip on power is weakening, and that the people of Iran are increasingly willing to take to the streets to voice their discontent.

On the international stage, Pezeshkian has shown no deviation from the regime's entrenched foreign policy, which is rooted in hostility towards the West and unwavering support for terrorist proxies. His silence in the face of escalating Houthi attacks on commercial shipping in the Red Sea, Hezbollah's provocations along Israel's northern border, and Iran's drone exports to Russia speaks volumes. Far from being a moderating force, Pezeshkian has echoed the Supreme Leader's anti-Western rhetoric and reaffirmed Iran's commitment to "strategic depth," a doctrine that justifies exporting revolution through militias and asymmetric warfare. His presidency, therefore, not only serves to suppress dissent at home but to reinforce the regime's destabilising ambitions abroad.

Alireza Kazemi, the Minister of Education in Masoud Pezeshkian's cabinet, has deployed police forces to schools to suppress students. During a joint meeting between the police and the Ministry of Education on 20 April 2025, Kazemi addressed Brigadier General Ahmad Reza Radan, the Commander of the regime's police force, stating: "In every field, I am Commander Radan's soldier. I proudly say he is a beloved and admirable figure in our country, someone we are proud of... Consider us your soldiers. Any mission you think we can carry out jointly in this field, we are at your service. The Ministry of Education is at your full disposal... Together, we will carry out important tasks. One of the greatest and most serious threats facing the country is the issue of social harm."[147]

Pezeshkian's presidency has confirmed what millions of Iranians already knew, that power in the Islamic Republic lies not in the ballot box, but in the hands of the unelected Supreme Leader. Far from heralding

---

[147] Official Collaboration Between the Ministry of Education and Security Forces to Suppress Students," Iran Human Rights Monitor, 24 April 2025. Available at: https://iran-hrm.com/2025/04/24/official-collaboration-between-the-ministry-of-education-and-security-forces-to-suppress-students/

reform, Pezeshkian has dutifully followed the script written for him by Khamenei, enforcing ideological purges and suppressing dissent with ruthless efficiency. Yet in doing so, he has exposed the regime's deepest fear: a well-informed, educated, and defiant population. The mass rejection of his presidency, the ongoing protests in the streets, and the unwavering defiance of students and teachers all signal that this regime of puppetry and repression is running out of strings. The future of Iran will not be written by those who cling to power through fear, but by those who dare to imagine and demand something better.

16

"Rebellion to tyrants is obedience to God."
- *Thomas Jefferson*

FROM PROTEST TO REVOLUTION: THE RISE OF RESISTANCE IN IRAN

Since the 1979 Iranian Revolution, which led to the establishment of the theocracy, Iran has experienced multiple nationwide uprisings and significant protests. While the initial impetus for some of these protests may have centred around more limited demands for expanded freedoms, they quickly evolved into broader calls for the regime's complete overthrow. These have included the 1999 Student Protests, which according to The New York Times, "shook" Iran's government in just two days.[148] The report added: "One day after a violent police raid on a Tehran University dormitory, more than 10,000 students demonstrated here and in other Iranian

---

[148] "Student Protests Shake Iran's Government," The New York Times, 11 July 1999. Available at:
https://www.nytimes.com/1999/07/11/world/student-protests-shake-iran-s-government.html

cities today, chanting slogans against government hard-liners and clashing at times with the police."[149]

Seeds of Revolt: Early Protests and Regime Resistance

Although self-proclaimed "reformists" initially sought to leverage the protests as a means to negotiate greater influence within the existing political structure, the students' intensifying demands for regime change compelled these actors to reconsider their strategy, wary of the broader implications leading to the regime's overthrow. President Mohammad Khatami, billed as a "reformist" or "moderate" in the West, called this evolution of protests into regime change "a deviation," and said in a fiery speech designed to curry favour with Supreme Leader Khamenei on 13 July 1999: "A Day or two after the events on Thursday night [8 July], a deviation took place. The aim was to inflict damage to the *foundation of the system* (regime)."[150] He added: "The issues raised, slogans chanted - inflammatory slogans against the values of the system ... are all meant to create divisions. ... Our noble nation will not be deceived by these slogans."[151]

Other "reformists" quickly followed suit to avoid further damage to the "foundation of the system." On

---

[149] Ibid.
[150] "Full text of Khatami's speech" BBC, 15 July 1999. Available at: http://news.bbc.co.uk/2/hi/world/monitoring/393909.stm
[151] Ibid.

14 July, an official rally was held in Tehran. Supreme National Security Council secretary and future "reformist" president - Hassan Rouhani, told the crowd that "those involved in the last days' riots and ... attacks against the system [regime] will be tried and punished as *mohareb* [those at war with God] and [those spreading corruption]."[152]

Similarly, in 2009, "the most intense protests in a decade" were initially triggered by allegations of election fraud in the presidential election.[153] However, they quickly morphed into calls for the regime's complete overthrow. Just three days after the initial protest, media reported, "Several vehicles were set on fire in Tehran's streets and there were reports that protesters had taken to city rooftops at nightfall, shouting 'Death to the dictator'", referring to the regime's Supreme Leader Ali Khamenei.[154]

A week after the first day of protests, footage of a 26-year-old female protester, Neda Agha Soltan, dying

---

[152] "Iran Report: July 19, 1999", Radio Free Europe, 19 July 1999, Vol. 2, No. 29. Available at:
https://www.rferl.org/a/1342937.html
[153] "Protests Flare in Tehran as Opposition Disputes Vote", The New York Times, 13 June 2009. Available at:
https://www.nytimes.com/2009/06/14/world/middleeast/14iran.html
[154] "Iran uprising turns bloody", The Guardian, 16 June 2009. Available at:
https://www.theguardian.com/world/2009/jun/15/iran-elections-protests-mousavi-attacks

after being shot, was seen around the world.[155] Conservative estimates, including those reported by human rights group Amnesty International, indicated, "thousands of people were arbitrarily arrested, dozens were killed on the streets or died in detention, and many said they were tortured or otherwise ill-treated."[156]

In the end, the people, undeterred by the authorities' brutality, called for the complete overthrow of the regime. By December, the Los Angeles Times reported: "News of chaos and fierce clashes continue to pour out from Tehran, with some on the Web describing the city as a war zone. ... It is said [security forces] lost control in certain parts [of the capital] and been pushed away by crowds of protesters."[157] In January 2011, the regime accused two activists of the PMOI, which has long called for the theocracy's complete overthrow, of orchestrating the 2009 protests and executed them.[158]

---

[155] "Iranian says militiaman killed protester", NBC News, 25 June 2009. Available at:
https://www.nbcnews.com/id/wbna31551388
[156] "Iran: Election contested, repression compounded", Amnesty International, 10 December 2009.
https://www.amnesty.org/en/documents/mde13/123/2009/en/
[157] "IRAN: Even more footage, pictures from Ashura protests", LA Times, 27 December 2009. Available at:
https://www.latimes.com/archives/blogs/babylon-beyond/story/2009-12-27/iran-even-more-footage-pictures-from-ashura-protests
[158] "Government hangs two activists condemned for post-election protests", Agence France Presse, 24 January 2011. Available at:

Revolution Rising: Organized Resistance and Nationwide Defiance

Since then, protests have become much more focused on the regime's overthrow and progressively more organised. In December 2017 and January 2018, Iran experienced a massive nationwide uprising that spread across all 31 provinces and over 142 cities.[159] This uprising was a turning point in the struggle against 40 years of theocratic rule in Iran. According to the Washington Post: "The scale and ferocity of the protests had clerical leaders in Tehran struggling Tuesday to respond to what is likely the most serious internal crisis the country has faced this decade". [160]

Despite the clerical regime's extensive efforts to suppress the protests, including killings and executions, the discontent continued to simmer, leading to ongoing demonstrations throughout the

---

https://www.france24.com/en/20110124-government-hangs-two-activists-condemned-2009-post-election-protests

[159] A senior Iranian regime official and former intelligence officer, Ali Rabii, even went further and said that people protested in 160 cities across the country. See the state-run ISNA report, 13 January 2019. Available at:
https://www.isna.ir/news/97102211876/علی-ربیعی-مدارای-بزرگ-استراتژی-دولت-در-اعتراضات-۹۶-بود

[160] "Tens of thousands of people have protested in Iran. Here's why", The Washington Post, 3 January 2018. Available at: https://www.washingtonpost.com/news/worldviews/wp/2018/01/03/tens-of-thousands-of-people-protested-in-iran-this-week-heres-why/

year. The dire economic conditions, caused by decades of deeply rooted corruption and mismanagement, plunged the majority of Iranians into poverty. Even official statistics, often manipulated in the regime's favour, indicated that the inflation rate in Iran surged from over 10% in 2017 to 31.2% in 2018, with projections at the time to reach 41.2% in 2019.[161]

The initial wave of protests in December 2017 saw massive participation across the country, with demonstrators calling for the overthrow of the clerical regime. They were followed by uprisings in January, May,[162] June,[163] September,[164] October,[165]

---

[161] Central Bank of the Islamic Republic of Iran, Available at: https://www.cbi.ir/
[162] "Iran's Striking Truckers Jolt Government into Addressing Grievances", Voice of America, 24 May 2018. Available at: https://www.voanews.com/a/iranian-truck-driver-protests/4407715.html
[163] "Iran's power struggle plays out in Tehran's Grand Bazaar", CNN, 27 June 2018. Available at: https://www.cnn.com/2018/06/27/middleeast/iran-protests-analysis-intl/index.html
[164] "Iranian Truckers Launch Another Strike to Protest Rising Costs ", Voice of America, 26 September 2018. Available at: https://www.voanews.com/a/iranian-truckers-launch-another-prolonged-strike-to-protest-rising-costs/4589270.html
[165] "Teachers' Strike Sees Classes Canceled Across Iran", Radio Farda, 15 October 2018. Available at: https://en.radiofarda.com/a/iran-nationwide-teachers-strike-wages-living-standards/29544285.html

November,[166] and December[167] of 2018 in several major provinces, with different strata of society, including truck drivers, teachers, Bazaar merchants, workers, farmers, and retirees, expressing their local and national grievances, all of which coalesced around the call for regime change.

As expected, the regime relied heavily on suppression, killings, and executions to stifle dissent.[168] However, the protests revealed the regime's vulnerability and isolation, both domestically and internationally. The 2017-2018 uprising was marked by the emergence and active participation of organised resistance units of the PMOI as a relatively new phenomenon.[169] The

---

[166] "Iran: Mounting Crackdown on Teachers, Labor Activists", Human Rights Watch, 22 November 2018. Available at: https://www.hrw.org/news/2018/11/22/iran-mounting-crackdown-teachers-labor-activists

[167] "Ahvaz Workers Continue Protests, Calling Rulers 'Thieves'", Radio Farda, 4 December 2018. Available at: https://en.radiofarda.com/a/iran-steel-workers-continue-protests-in-ahvaz/29636780.html

[168] See, for example: "Iran: Executions of three Iranian Kurds an outrage", Amnesty International, 8 September 2018. Available at: https://www.amnesty.org/en/latest/press-release/2018/09/iran-executions-of-three-iranian-kurds-an-outrage/

[169] Most notably, the protests were fuelled by Resistance Units allied with the main opposition PMOI/PMOI. On December 2, 2018, the state-run Qaboos Nameh wrote: "The recent (2017/2018) protests were the continuation of failed riots of December (2017) led by the PMOI. The PMOI infiltrates legitimate protest gatherings of the people, using its agents that it calls 'Resistance Units.'" Available at (in Farsi): http://qaboosnameh.ir/news/7563/-واكاوي-نقش-منافقين-در-حركات اعتراضي-اقشار-جامعه-يادداشت

organised opposition's crucial role in recent years has been acknowledged by the regime. Mahmoud Alavi, the former Minister of Intelligence and Security (MOIS), admitted in early 2019: "Over the past year, 116 teams associated with the PMOI have been dealt with."[170]

In 2024, PMOI resistance units hacked regime billboards in Mashhad to display "Death to the Dictator" and distributed 10,000 anti-regime leaflets in Tabriz, galvanizing public dissent, as reported by Iran International (2024).

The most important takeaway from the 2017-2018 protests was the overwhelming rejection of all the regime's factions, particularly "hardliners" and "reformists."[171] For many years, the narrative of "reformists" vs. "hardliners" was used by the Supreme Leader with two objectives: Channelling the growing popular discontent at home into possible change from within the regime, which remained under his own control; and on the international level to maintain the illusion of reform from within the regime. The protests demonstrated the resilience of the Iranian

---

[170] State-run Fars News Agency, 19 April 2019.
[171] Majid Rafizadeh, "Iran Protests: "Reformists, Hardliner, The Game is Now Over"", Huffington Post, 30 December 2017. Available at: https://www.huffpost.com/entry/iran-protests-reformists-hardliner-game-is-over_b_5a47fb0ee4b0df0de8b06aac

people and their determination to fight for their rights despite severe repression.

Tehran, Resistance Units hang a poster of Iranian opposition leader Maryam Rajavi from an overpass. The writing says: "Our choice is Maryam Rajavi." (Photo: PMOI)

Additionally, they highlighted the significant influence of the organised opposition. This impact was so pronounced that a visibly shaken Supreme Leader - Ali Khamenei, publicly recognised their role in the uprisings. Khamenei said in a speech on January 9, 2018: "The third angle of the triangle consists of the U.S. submissive henchmen: Mujahedin-e Khalq Organisation, the murderous PMOI. They were prepared months ago. The media of the PMOI admitted to this: to organise riots, meet with this or that person, find individuals inside the country to help them fan out to the people. And that it was they who initiated this.... They began with a slogan [to catch attention] in opposition to high prices. Well, this is a slogan that everyone likes. They wanted to attract some people with this message, then enter the arena themselves to pursue their evil goals and attract followers. What people did here is this: they came to (the) streets."[172]

A steep increase in fuel prices sparked the 2020 Fuel Price Protests that spread nationwide. According to media reports, Iran experienced "its deadliest political unrest since the Islamic Revolution 40 years ago."[173] The government response was harsh, with significant loss of life and mass arrests. The November 2019 uprising, driven by economic grievances and demands for regime change, once again challenged the mullahs' authority in an unprecedented manner. The regime's response was brutal: a severe crackdown ordered by Supreme Leader Ali Khamenei resulted in over 1,500 deaths and numerous injuries and arrests.[174] Despite this repression, the gains from the uprising are seen as irreversible, highlighting persistent unrest and the regime's inherent weaknesses.

---

[172] Ali Khamenei's meeting with the people of Qom, 9 January 2018. Available at: https://english.khamenei.ir/news/5397/The-people-have-always-entered-the-arena-whenever-the-country

[173] "With Brutal Crackdown, Iran Is Convulsed by Worst Unrest in 40 Years", The New York Times, 3 December 2019. Available at: https://www.nytimes.com/2019/12/01/world/middleeast/iran-protests-deaths.html

[174] "Special Report: Iran's leader ordered crackdown on unrest - 'Do whatever it takes to end it'", Reuters, 23 December 2019. Available at: https://www.reuters.com/article/world/special-report-irans-leader-ordered-crackdown-on-unrest-do-whatever-it-take-idUSKBN1YR0QO/

The protests were characterized by anti-regime slogans and significant participation across major cities like Tehran, Mashhad, Isfahan, and Shiraz. The regime's deployment of extensive resources, including the IRGC and State Security Force (SSF), underscored its fear of losing control. The crackdown involved coordinated efforts across various provinces, with local commanders playing significant roles in the repression. The scale of the suppression only fuelled public outrage, further igniting the protests. A particularly brutal crackdown occurred in Mahshahr, in southern Iran, where security forces used heavy machine guns and helicopters to quell protests, resulting in numerous deaths that included women and children.[175]

Supreme Leader Ali Khamenei, President Hassan Rouhani, and IRGC commanders were central to the suppression. The protesters also rejected both the regime's theocracy and the former monarchical dictatorship of the Shah prior to the 1979 anti-monarchical revolution. Once again, the Iranian regime accused the PMOI of leading the protests,

---

[175] "Exclusive: Eyewitness Describes Brutal Attack On Iran Protesters In Mahshahr", Radio Farda, 11 December 2019. Available at: https://en.radiofarda.com/a/exclusive-eyewitness-describes-brutal-attack-on-iran-protesters-in-mahshahr/30319712.html

pointing to a well- organised opposition that has long been a thorn in the regime's side.[176]

Hossein Ashtari, the Commander of State Security Forces (SSF), said: "Our investigations show that behind the scenes, anti-revolutionary organizations and the PMOI led these movements. The country's security and law enforcement entities have identified these individuals, and God willing, they will be punished for their actions at the right time."[177] This highlighted the ongoing struggle between the regime and organised resistance movement, which continues to challenge the mullahs' authority despite severe repression.

In a televised speech on 8 January 2020, Khamenei accused the PMOI of leading the 2019 protests: "Several days before the [2019] uprising, in a small and sinister country in Europe [Albania, home to the PMOI's headquarters] an American and a number of Iranians [PMOI] drew up plans, which we saw in the gasoline incident. As soon as (protesting) people came to the scene, the enemy's operatives began. Demolishing, torching, murder, destroy, and foment war. This was a renewal of the work they had carried

---

[176] The Supreme Leader, Ali Khamenei, said in a televised speech on 17 November 2019: "In the course of such incidents, usually thugs, spiteful individuals, and unsavoury people enter the scene. ... the wicked and criminal collective of the PMOI, they are constantly encouraging and inviting people on social networks and elsewhere to conduct these evil acts."
[177] State-run Fars News Agency, 17 November 2019.

out before. And they continue to take these actions, and they will do whatever they can."[178]

The November 2019 uprising highlighted the need for robust international measures to support the Iranian people's quest for freedom and to hold the regime accountable for its crimes. Moreover, what distinguished the 2019 protests was the significant involvement of the poor, the underprivileged, and the downtrodden sectors of society, long, albeit mistakenly, perceived by analysts as the backbone of the regime's support.

This participation marked a crucial shift in the socio-political landscape of Iran, indicating that the regime's base of presumed support was eroding. The active participation of these marginalized groups not only expanded the demographic reach of the protests but also underscored the deep-seated discontent permeating all levels of Iranian society.

This widespread dissatisfaction explained the ferocious nature of the uprising, as hundreds of regime centres, government-controlled banks, IRGC bases, and other government agencies were torched and destroyed by throngs of enraged citizens. The targeting of the IRGC and other repressive forces by

---

[178] "Albanian Leaders Dismiss Khamenei's Purported 'Sinister' Smear", Radio Free Europe, 9 January 2020. Available at: https://www.rferl.org/a/albanian-leaders-dismiss-khamenei-s-purported-sinister-smear/30368335.html

the protesters highlighted the intensity of their anger and the breadth of their grievances against the state apparatus, signalling a significant escalation in the methods and aims of public dissent.

In 2021 there were a series of Drought Protests, particularly in the southwestern province of Khuzestan, where severe water shortages had been caused by environmental mismanagement.[179] Then in 2021/2022 teachers across the country protested demanding better wages and working conditions.[180]

On 16 September 2022, the tragic death of Mahsa (Jina) Amini, a 22-year-old woman from Saqqez, Kurdistan province, while in the custody of the "Morality Police," sparked another wave of widespread protests across Iran that had been growing in strength since 2017.[181] The uprising quickly spread across the country to 300 cities. Women led 40% of the 2022 protest actions, organizing schoolgirl

---

[179] "Thousands rally in central Iran to protest water shortages", Reuters, 19 November 2021. Available at: https://www.reuters.com/markets/commodities/thousands-rally-central-iran-protest-water-shortages-2021-11-19/
[180] "Tehran clamps down on teachers", Deutsche Welle, 4 October 2021. Available at: https://www.dw.com/en/iran-clamps-down-on-teachers-demanding-fair-pay/a-59401317
[181] "Iran: Deadly crackdown on protests against Mahsa Amini's death in custody needs urgent global action", Amnesty International, 21 September 2022. Available at: https://www.amnesty.org/en/latest/news/2022/09/iran-deadly-crackdown-on-protests-against-mahsa-aminis-death-in-custody-needs-urgent-global-action/

walkouts and hijab-burning rallies, as noted by Amnesty International (2023).[182]

Iran's economic situation in 2022 was dire, with a 50% surge in the cost of living, a plummeting currency, and soaring food prices. These economic hardships, in conjunction with the regime's political suppression, acted as a catalyst for the protests, exacerbating the existing political and social grievances. These protests saw unprecedented participation from various segments of society, including the middle class, merchants, the impoverished working class, and even traditional conservative groups.

Women and young people were at the forefront, highlighting a broad-based discontent with the regime's oppressive policies. Protesters chanted slogans such as "Death to the oppressor, be it the Shah or the Supreme Leader," and "Death to the dictator." [183] These slogans encapsulated the protesters' broad discontent with authoritarian rule and their desire for a democratic republic. More notably, credible accounts indicated that once again, the main organised resistance movement played a decisive role

---

[182] Amnesty International, "Iran: Women Lead 2022 Uprisings," March 2023.
[183] "What to Know About the Iranian Protests Over Mahsa Amini's Death", Time Magazine, 24 September 2022. Available at: https://time.com/6216513/mahsa-amini-iran-protests-police/

in organising, leading, expanding, and sustaining the uprisings.[184]

By 2024, inflation soared to 45%, and the rial lost 70% of its value since 2022, pushing 60% of Iranians below the poverty line, according to the World Bank.[185] In early 2025, Iran's revolutionary fervour intensified as economic collapse fuelled a new wave of protests across 100 cities, with 50,000 demonstrators in Tehran alone chanting "Down with Khamenei" on March 10, as reported by Radio Farda (2025). PMOI resistance units amplified the uprising, projecting anti-regime slogans on Shiraz's municipal buildings and disabling IRGC surveillance in Isfahan, escalating defiance against the regime's crackdowns, per opposition sources (NCRI, 2025).[186] In the Iranian year ending March 20, 2025, PMOI resistance units conducted thousands of operations against IRGC and Basij targets, including torching regime symbols and

---

[184] Attempting to discourage university students to join the ranks of the Resistance Units, the regime's former president Ebrahim Raisi said in a speech to a group of Sharif University officials on 6 October 2022: "We are sure that the Sharif students will not allow ill-wishers and Hypocrites [PMOI] to distort this university." See State-affiliated Farda News, 6 October 2022. Available at (in Farsi): https://www.fardanews.com/بخش-سیاست-۷۳/۱۱۷۸٤٤٠-رئیسی-نباید-اعتبار-علمی-دانشگاه-شریف-با-رفتارهای-تحمیلی-از-بیرون-مخدوش-شود

[185] World Bank, "Iran Economic Update: Inflation and Poverty Surge," June 2024.

[186] Radio Farda, "Iran Faces Nationwide Protests Amid Economic Crisis," 12 March 2025; NCRI, "Resistance Units Lead 2025 Uprisings," 15 March 2025.

projecting resistance messages, as reported by opposition sources.[187]

John F Kennedy famously said: *"Those who make peaceful revolution impossible will make violent revolution inevitable".*[188] His words should resonate in Tehran today. For forty-six years the Iranian regime has sponsored violent abduction, hostage taking, kidnapping, blackmail, piracy, assassination, warmongering and oppression. As a gangster regime, the theocratic dictatorship has no equal.

Despite the regime's relentless brutality, the Iranian people have shown time and again that their thirst for freedom cannot be extinguished. From students and teachers to workers and pensioners, from women defiantly removing their hijabs to youths facing down armed security forces, the message is unmistakable: the era of religious dictatorship is drawing to a close.

The nationwide uprisings of recent years have not only exposed the deep fractures within the regime but also revealed the strength, courage, and organisation

---

[187] "Persian Year 1403: A Year of Tumult for the Regime and Transformation for Iran," The National Council of Resistance of Iran, March 20, 2025. Available at: http://ncr-iran.org/en/news/iran-resistance/persian-year-1403-a-year-of-tumult-and-transformation-for-iran/
[188] President John F. Kennedy, "Remarks on the first anniversary of the Alliance for Progress, 13 March 1962. Available at: https://www.goodreads.com/quotes/89101-those-who-make-peaceful-revolution-impossible-will-make-violent-revolution

of a society ready to reclaim its future. In the Iranian new year that ended on March 20, 2025, the Resistance Units carried out 3,007 operations against the bases and centres of the IRGC, the paramilitary Basij, and other regime security and suppressive organs. They also conducted 39,000 acts of defiance, torching regime symbols, such as portraits of regime leaders, the eliminated Quds Force commander Qassem Soleimani, unfurling banners with pictures of the Iranian Resistance's leadership from overpasses or projecting them on high rise buildings.[189] With the organised resistance gaining momentum[190] and the cries for justice echoing louder in every corner of the nation, the day is fast approaching when the Iranian people will consign both the monarchy and the theocracy to the pages of history, and finally build a democratic, secular republic founded on freedom, equality, and the rule of law.

---

[189] Resistance Units X account, https://x.com/ResistanceUnits/status/1904934212261622036
[190] "Persian Year 1403: A Year of Tumult for the Regime and Transformation for Iran," The National Council of Resistance of Iran, March 20, 2025. Available at: http://ncr-iran.org/en/news/iran-resistance/persian-year-1403-a-year-of-tumult-and-transformation-for-iran/

17

"Dictators ride to and fro on tigers from which they dare not dismount. And the tigers are getting hungry."
- Winston Churchill

THE FINAL RECKONING: IRAN AT THE EDGE OF CHANGE

This book has chronicled the grim realities of Iran's theocratic regime, but also the unyielding spirit of its people. As we now draw together the threads of these harrowing yet hopeful narratives, one truth shines through: the Islamic Republic is a regime in sharp decline, sustained not by the will of the people, but by terror, repression, and deceit. The Iranian people, having endured four and a half decades of despotism, stand once more on the cusp of profound transformation.

The clerical regime highjacked the revolution of millions of Iranians who wanted a free, just, and independent republic, but this regime brought about this subjugation by kidnapping the leadership. The monarchy's fall in 1979 could have opened the gates to a secular, democratic republic. Instead, it paved the way for the clerics to seize power through violence and deception. The doctrine of *velayat-e faqih*, the absolute guardianship of the Islamic jurist, emerged as the legal and philosophical scaffold for a regime that brooks no dissent, no deviation, and tolerates no alternative legitimacy. In Khomeini's Iran, and now under Khamenei's tyranny, opposition is criminalized, often punishable by death.

Iran became a nation ruled not by law, but by decree. Its institutions serve the Supreme Leader, not the citizen. Its show trials convict before hearing evidence. Its elections are charades. Dissent is met with torture, imprisonment, or execution. Women are treated as second-class citizens, subjected to medieval rules and brutal enforcement by morality police. Ethnic and religious minorities are denied equality and representation. Students are expelled, lecturers purged, journalists jailed, artists silenced.

Yet perhaps the regime's most insidious crime has been the theft of hope, particularly from its youth. This is a young country, yet dreams of opportunity and progress are consistently crushed beneath the boot of ideological dogma and corruption. Iran's bright, educated generation finds itself stifled in a system where connections to the IRGC matter more than merit; where clerics rule science, and mullahs dictate morality.

And while repression at home has intensified, the regime has squandered Iran's wealth and reputation abroad. Billions of dollars have been poured into a sprawling network of militias and terror outfits, Hezbollah, the Houthis, Hamas, Shi'ite militias in Iraq and Syria, all designed to project Iranian power and ideology across the region. Tehran's axis of resistance has destabilised countries in the region, prolonged wars, and sowed the seeds of sectarian hatred from Baghdad to Beirut. This is a regime whose fingerprints are found on the wreckage of collapsed states and failed ceasefires.

The consequences for ordinary Iranians have been catastrophic. Despite the country's immense natural resources, the economy lies in ruins. Inflation rages. Corruption is endemic. Jobs are scarce, the currency is worthless, and millions live below the poverty line. Yet the IRGC thrives, commanding an empire of illicit trade, drug trafficking, construction contracts, and military industries. The regime's cronies prosper while the people queue for bread and medicine.

But repression can only smother dissent for so long. Across four and a half decades, Iran has been rocked by wave after wave of protest, each more widespread and defiant than the last. These are not isolated eruptions. They are a continuum of resistance. They are the heartbeat of a nation that remembers its dignity and refuses to be broken. In 1999, students rose. In 2009, voters cried foul. In 2017, the impoverished demanded justice. In 2019, the fuel hikes ignited fury. In 2022, the murder of Mahsa Amini became the spark for a generational revolt.

And in these uprisings, a pattern has emerged: chants once aimed at reform have become calls for regime change. "Death to the dictator." "Neither Shah nor Mullah." "We want a republic, not a theocracy." These are not slogans, they are manifestos.

A striking feature of recent uprisings has been the role of organised, disciplined networks known as Resistance Units. These courageous men and women, inspired by the People's Mojahedin Organisation of Iran (PMOI or MEK), have moved beyond protest to active civil resistance. They disable surveillance systems, set fire to regime symbols, expose human rights violations, and amplify the voices of dissent across digital and physical platforms. Their tools are courage and coordination.

This form of resistance has proven to be very effective and terrible for the regime. It is calculated. It is flexible. It is resilient. It is nationwide. It is, in short, the regime's worst nightmare: an organised opposition capable of strategic disruption. It is this same organised resistance, under the broader umbrella of the National Council of Resistance of Iran (NCRI), that offers a viable path forward. Led by Maryam Rajavi, the NCRI has put forth a clear and credible political platform: a ten-point plan for a democratic Iran, grounded in universal suffrage, secularism, gender equality, the abolition of the death penalty, and peaceful coexistence. It calls for a republic founded on the rule of law, not the rule of clerics. And it is gaining traction. Across many parliaments in Europe, in the U.S. Congress, and among former world leaders, support for the NCRI and its vision has grown exponentially.[191]

Brussels, 20 Nov. 2024 - Maryam Rajavi addresses the European Parliament and lays out a roadmap for the transfer of power to the Iranian people. (Photo: NCRI)

The year 2025 marked a decisive shift in international solidarity with the Iranian people's fight for

---

[191] "4,000 lawmakers in 50 countries to support Maryam Rajavi's 10-Point Plan, MEK resistance units," The Washington Times, 27 June 2024. Available at:
https://www.washingtontimes.com/news/2024/jun/27/4000-lawmakers-in-50-countries-to-support-maryam-r/

democracy and human rights. Three landmark achievements, in Spain, the United States, and the United Kingdom, highlighted the growing global support for the Iranian resistance, particularly the National Council of Resistance of Iran (NCRI) and its President-elect, Maryam Rajavi. The Iranian regime's panicked reactions to these developments underlined its growing vulnerability and the increasing legitimacy of the democratic alternative.

On 6 May 2025, the Foreign Affairs Committee of the Spanish Parliament unanimously adopted a resolution condemning the Iranian regime's grave human rights abuses. Proposed by the Popular Party (PP) and supported by all parliamentary groups, the resolution cited NCRI reports documenting over 1,000 executions in 2024, the highest figure in decades. The resolution condemned systematic torture, extrajudicial killings, and institutionalised discrimination against women, especially through veiling laws and the draconian "Hijab and Chastity Law".

It also referenced individual cases such as those of political prisoners Mehdi Hassani and Behrouz Ehsani, both sentenced to death for their alleged association with the PMOI. The Spanish Parliament commended the NCRI's international advocacy efforts, notably a large opposition rally in Paris on 8 February 2025 and Maryam Rajavi's keynote address at the International Women's Conference.

Shortly thereafter, on 14 May, the U.S. House of Representatives passed House Resolution 166 with 224 co-sponsors from both the Republican and Democratic parties, a rare moment of bipartisan unity. The resolution expressed support for the Iranian people's desire to establish a democratic, secular, and non-nuclear republic. It endorsed Maryam Rajavi's Ten-Point Plan and recognised the Iranian people's right to resist tyranny.

The resolution condemned the regime's role in terrorism and destabilisation across the region, as well as its ongoing human rights abuses, including the execution of more than 500 individuals in 2025 alone. It further called for international recognition of the NCRI as a viable democratic alternative.

On 17 May 2025, a cross-party conference held in Paris saw the unprecedented endorsement of 560 members of the UK Parliament for a new policy on Iran. This broad coalition included current and former cabinet ministers, party leaders, and peers from across the political spectrum. Their joint statement urged the UK government to designate the Islamic Revolutionary Guard Corps (IRGC) as a terrorist entity and to support the Iranian people's democratic aspirations.

The Iranian regime reacted with predictable panic. State media unleashed a barrage of attacks on the NCRI and its supporters, attempting to discredit the resolutions and the lawmakers behind them. The regime's Foreign Ministry summoned ambassadors from Spain and the UK in protest. Friday prayer sermons, often used to disseminate regime propaganda, denounced Western parliaments for "interference" and accused them of "collusion with terrorists", a term it routinely applies to the PMOI.

On state television, officials accused Maryam Rajavi of orchestrating these initiatives and warned of "consequences" for those promoting "anti-revolutionary plots". The regime launched cyber-attacks on websites affiliated with the NCRI and intensified its disinformation campaigns on Western media platforms.

Yet the opposition has endured. Unlike monarchists who pine for a past that never delivered freedom, the NCRI offers a future anchored in modernity, accountability, and inclusion. The monarchist movement, led by Reza Pahlavi, has increasingly functioned not as a force for change, but as a useful tool for the regime. Cloaked in ultranationalist rhetoric and neo-fascist imagery, it revives a whitewashed version of the Shah's rule, ignoring the corruption, repression, and brutality of the SAVAK that helped spark the 1979 revolution. Far from presenting a credible alternative, it alienates Iranians who reject both monarchy and theocracy.

Rather than challenge the regime, the monarchists provide it with a convenient foil. Their divisive narrative damages the opposition, weakens grassroots resistance, and allows the mullahs to claim that all alternatives are either extremist or nostalgic. The Islamic Republic has long used figures like Pahlavi to muddy the waters and discredit genuine democratic forces. In truth, this monarchist revival is not a threat to the regime, it is one of its greatest assets.

The world has witnessed the fall of dictatorships once thought unassailable. Adolf Hitler and his fascist friend Benito Mussolini thought that they could rule the world. Hitler even declared that he was the founder of a "Thousand Year Reich." It lasted only 12 years. The collapse of the Soviet Union in 1991 marked the end of decades of dictatorship under the Communist Party.

Popular uprisings, economic instability, and political reforms led to the dissolution of the Soviet regime and the emergence of independent governments in former Soviet republics. Beginning in late 2010, a series of protests and demonstrations across the Middle East and North Africa led to the downfall of several long-standing dictatorships, such as in Tunisia, Egypt, Libya, and Yemen. Citizens rose up against authoritarian rulers, demanding political freedoms, economic reforms, and social justice.

In 1986, a popular uprising known as the 'People Power Revolution' ousted the dictator Ferdinand Marcos, who had ruled the Philippines for over two decades. Mass protests, civil disobedience, and the support of the military played a crucial role in ending his authoritarian rule. In December 1989, popular unrest and mass demonstrations culminated in the overthrow and execution of the Romanian dictator Nicolae Ceausescu. The fall of the Ceausescu regime marked the end of decades of oppressive communist rule in Romania.

Through a combination of international pressure, internal resistance, and negotiations, the apartheid regime in South Africa under President F.W. de Klerk was dismantled, paving the way for democratic elections in 1994 and the election of Nelson Mandela as the country's first black president.

These examples highlight the power of popular movements, international pressure, internal dissent, and diplomatic efforts in bringing about the downfall of dictatorships and the transition to more democratic forms of governance. The sudden and unexpected ousting of Bashar al-Assad in Syria in December 2024 was a further example of the power of the people when they are willing to risk everything to overthrow a tyrant.

All of these essential elements are in place to end the mullahs' gangster regime in Iran. Coordinated acts of defiance now define the daily rhythm of resistance. Across Iran, the people have reclaimed the narrative. They no longer speak in whispers. They sing of liberty and scrawl it across walls. The tide has turned.

Women have not only led the chants of protest in Iran they have led the movement. From the schoolgirls to the imprisoned activists, to the organisers behind countless Resistance Units, Iranian women have transformed from victims of repression into architects of rebellion. They are not merely participating they are defining the shape of Iran's future.

This is no accident. The gender apartheid of the Islamic Republic has produced a counterforce just as powerful: a generation of women who understand that true liberation is against Islamic Fundamentalism. Any democratic Iran will be shaped by their courage, and any vision of the future must recognise them not as accessories to change, but as its leaders.

A democratic Iran would not only free its people it would shift the gravitational centre of the Middle East. A nation once synonymous with oppression and export of extremism would become a beacon of pluralism, peace, and progress. It would send shockwaves through every autocracy in the region, giving renewed strength to democratic movements from Beirut to Baghdad. It would bring stability to global markets, reduce the threat of nuclear escalation, and curtail the spread of terrorism. More importantly, it would prove, again, that when people rise with unity, vision, and unbreakable will, they can redraw the map not just of a nation, but of an entire region.

The regime is afraid. And it should be. Not of foreign armies, but of its own people. No amount of propaganda, no flood of executions, no wave of arrests can hide the truth: the people have withdrawn their consent. The social contract has been shattered. What remains is a brittle dictatorship, paranoid and paralysed.

The international community now stands at a moral crossroads. For too long, Western governments have clung to a policy of appeasement, offering concessions, signing flawed nuclear deals, ignoring the regime's terrorism and repression, and shunning the organised opposition. This approach has failed. It has emboldened the regime, prolonged the suffering of the Iranian people, and jeopardised global security.

It is time to reverse course. The regime's nuclear dossier must be referred to the UN Security Council. Sanctions should be reinstated, not lifted. The IRGC must be designated as a terrorist organisation by the UK and EU, as it already is in the U.S. and Canada. Iran's embassies, often nothing more than terror hubs, must be shut down. The regime's cyber warfare and hostage-taking diplomacy must be met with unified resistance. And above all, the NCRI and the Iranian people's right to resist must be recognised and supported.

A democratic Iran would be a game-changer, not only for Iranians but for the Middle East and the world. It would spell the end of the regime's terror networks. It would halt its nuclear blackmail. It would end its sectarian proxy wars. It would restore Iran to its rightful place among the community of civilised nations.

This book does not end in despair. It ends in defiance, and in the certainty that change is coming. Not through tanks or treaties, but through the determined efforts of a people who have had enough. Enough of lies. Enough of cruelty. Enough of fear.

Let the world not look away. Let the West no longer choose comfort over courage. Let history remember that when Iran stood on the brink of freedom, we stood with its people, not behind them, not above them, but beside them.

Because when the people rise, dictators fall.

PROFILE:

Struan Stevenson, member of European Parliament (1999 - 2014), President of the European Parliament's Delegation for Relations with Iraq (2009 - 2014), Chairman of the European Parliament Friends of a Free Iran Intergroup (2004 -2014), and Appointed Roving Ambassador to Central Asia by OSCE 2010. He is an author and international lecturer on the Middle East.

Other books by Struan Stevenson:

Printed in Dunstable, United Kingdom